Mitsubishi U

Safe.
73

BRAGGING RIGHTS

EVERY BLACK CATS VICTORY OVER THE MAGPIES

**Special thanks to
Paul Days and Bob Dixon**

Written by Brian Leng

A TWOCAN PUBLICATION

©2017. Published by twocan.
ISBN: 978-1-911502-53-1

Every effort has been made to ensure the accuracy of information within this publication but the publishers cannot be held responsible for any errors or omissions. Views expressed are those of the author and do not necessarily represent those of the publishers. All rights reserved.

PICTURES:
Action Images, Mirrorpix, Press Association.

FOREWORD

My earliest memory of supporting Sunderland was during the 1963-64 season when my mates and I would get the bus down from our homes in Annfield Plain, walk across Wearmouth Bridge and then head down Roker Avenue to the ground. I can clearly recall the feeling of excitement when we turned into Roker Baths Road and got out first glimpse of the ground and its towering floodlights.

I remember we used to race to the Fulwell End to try and get a perch on the fence at the back of the terracing where we could enjoy an uninterrupted view of the game. The turnstiles used to open at 1.30pm, so you needed to be there early to claim your spot, otherwise our lack of inches meant we would struggle to see much of the action.

I had certainly chosen the right season to add my weight to Sunderland's massive support, as the team were in brilliant form under the leadership of the legendary Charlie Hurley, winning promotion back to the top flight in style. They also enjoyed a great run in the FA Cup, beating League champions Everton before finally going out of the competition in the Sixth round after three epic games against Manchester United.

There were some brilliant games that season, but even at my tender age, I soon became acutely aware that there was one fixture that mattered more than any other - the Tyne-Wear derby against Newcastle United. These were the games where league form generally went out of the window, so high were the stakes on the North East football scene. Local pride was everything and to be able to go to school the next day after a victory was certainly something special as there were quite a number of Magpies where I lived and we took great delight in giving them stick. Mind you, we certainly suffered when the roles were reversed - there's no worse feeling than losing a derby match!

The first derby I saw was early in that 1963-64 season when a 2-1 victory helped keep Sunderland's Second Division promotion challenge on track. I remember Len Ashurst scored a 30-yarder that night, one of only four goals he scored in a massive career spanning 458 games! That was my first experience of the atmosphere and tension of a Tyne-Wear derby and one I would experience many times thereafter. Forget Manchester United, Chelsea and the rest, it's the Newcastle result that will always matter most to Sunderland fans!

Since their first victory back in April 1899, Sunderland have recorded 51 wins and each and every one is covered in detail in this book which features match reports, anecdotes from many of the players and managers involved as well as some great images.

It is a fascinating record of all those days when North East football's 'Bragging Rights' lay firmly in Wearside hands, from the fixture's earliest days right through to the record-breaking 'Six in a Row'. Over the years we have recorded many memorable victories over Newcastle and this book brings it all back to me. I hope it revives some great memories for you too.

MICKY HORSWILL

4	**Newcastle United 0-1 Sunderland** 22 April 1899, Division One
5	**Newcastle United 2-4 Sunderland** 23 December 1899, Division One
6	**Newcastle United 0-2 Sunderland** 24 April 1901, Division One
7	**Newcastle United 0-1 Sunderland** 28 September 1901, Division One
8	**Newcastle United 1-3 Sunderland** 26 December 1903, Division One
9	**Sunderland 3-1 Newcastle United** 24 December 1904, Division One
10	**Newcastle United 1-3 Sunderland** 22 April 1905, Division One
11	**Sunderland 3-2 Newcastle United** 2 September 1905, Division One
12	**Sunderland 2-0 Newcastle United** 20 March 1907, Division One
12	**Newcastle United 1-3 Sunderland** 18 April 1908, Division One
14	**Newcastle United 1-9 Sunderland** 5 December 1908, Division One
16	**Sunderland 3-1 Newcastle United** 10 April 1909, Division One
17	**Sunderland 2-1 Newcastle United** 1 September 1910, Division One
18	**Sunderland 2-0 Newcastle United** 28 December 1912, Division One
19	**Sunderland 0-0 Newcastle United** 8 March 1913, F.A.Cup Sixth Round
20	**Newcastle United 2-2 Sunderland** 12 March 1913, FA Cup Sixth Round Replay (AET)
21	**Newcastle United 0-3 Sunderland** 17 March 1913, FA Cup Sixth Round Second Replay
22	**Newcastle United 2-5 Sunderland** 25 December 1914, Division One

23	**Sunderland 2-0 Newcastle United** 22 November 1919, Division One	48	**Sunderland 2-1 Newcastle United** 9 October 1963, Division Two
24	**Newcastle United 2-3 Sunderland** 29 November 1919, Division One	50	**Sunderland 2-0 Newcastle United** 3 January 1966, Division One
25	**Sunderland 2-0 Newcastle United** 11 November 1922, Division One	51	**Newcastle United 0-3 Sunderland** 29 October 1966, Division One
26	**Sunderland 3-2 Newcastle United** 15 December 1923, Division One	52	**Sunderland 3-0 Newcastle United** 4 March 1967, Division One
27	**Newcastle United 0-2 Sunderland** 22 December 1923, Division One	54	**Newcastle United 1-4 Sunderland** 24 February 1979, Division Two
28	**Sunderland 2-0 Newcastle United** 30 October 1926, Division One	58	**Newcastle United 2-2 Sunderland** **Sunderland Won 7-6 on Penalties** 5 September 1979, League Cup Second Round Second Leg
29	**Sunderland 5-2 Newcastle United** 27 October 1928, Division One	60	**Sunderland 1-0 Newcastle United** 5 April 1980, Division Two
30	**Sunderland 1-0 Newcastle United** 19 October 1929, Division One	62	**Newcastle United 0-2 Sunderland** 16 May 1990, Division Two Play-Off Semi-Final Second Leg
30	**Sunderland 5-0 Newcastle United** 22 November 1930, Division One	66	**Newcastle United 1-2 Sunderland** 25 August 1999, Premier League
32	**Newcastle United 1-2 Sunderland** 9 April 1932, Division One	72	**Newcastle United 1-2 Sunderland** 18 November 2000, Premier League
33	**Newcastle United 0-1 Sunderland** 8 April 1933, Division One	76	**Sunderland 2-1 Newcastle United** 25 October 2008, Premier League
34	**Sunderland 2-0 Newcastle United** 3 March 1934, Division One	80	**Newcastle United 0-3 Sunderland** 14 April 2013, Premier League
36	**Sunderland 2-1 Newcastle United** 26 March 1951, Division One	84	**Sunderland 2-1 Newcastle United** 27 October 2013, Premier League
38	**Sunderland 4-2 Newcastle United** 9 October 1954, Division One	88	**Newcastle United 0-3 Sunderland** 1 February 2014, Premier League
39	**Newcastle United 1-2 Sunderland** 26 February 1955, Division One	92	**Newcastle United 0-1 Sunderland** 21 December 2014, Premier League
40	**Newcastle United 0-2 Sunderland** 3 March 1956, FA Cup Sixth Round	96	**Sunderland 1-0 Newcastle United** 5 April 2015, Premier League
44	**Sunderland 2-0 Newcastle United** 21 September 1957, Division One	102	**Sunderland 3-0 Newcastle United** 25 October 2015, Premier League
46	**Sunderland 3-0 Newcastle United** 21 April 1962, Division Two		

NEWCASTLE UNITED 0
SUNDERLAND 1
McLATCHIE

DATE: 22 April 1899
VENUE: St. James' Park
ATTENDANCE: 25,000
COMPETITION: League Division One
REFEREE: Mr. Lewis

NEWCASTLE UTD: Kingsley, Lindsay, Jackson, Ghee, Higgins, Aitken, Rogers, Stevenson, Peddie, McFarlane, Niblo.

SUNDERLAND: Doig, McCombie, McNeil, Wilson, McAllister, Raisbeck, Crawford, Leslie, Farquhar, Fulton, McLatchie.

The 1890s were a marvellous decade for Sunderland Football Club with the League Championship being lifted on no fewer than three occasions, a remarkable achievement that earned them the nickname 'The Team of all the Talents'.

Bearing in mind that success and having finished as runners-up the year before, the 1898-99 season has to go down as one of major disappointment for Sunderland with the club actually flirting with relegation at one point before finally finishing the campaign in a comfortable mid-table position. However, the season was particularly notable for the club's move to their new home at Roker Park as well as the first-ever Tyne-Wear derby matches, following Newcastle United's promotion to the First Division and, having lost to the Magpies on home soil earlier in the campaign, immediate revenge was very much on the minds of players and supporters alike as they headed up to Tyneside for the return fixture.

The game attracted huge interest with supporters flocking to St. James' Park which was soon packed to its 25,000 capacity with many fans scaling the rooftops of the adjacent Leazes Terrace to enjoy a free bird's-eye view of the game.

In those days the pitch had a pronounced slope and having won the toss, the home side elected play 'up the hill' in the first period.

The game quickly developed into an end-to-end encounter with both defences very much in command and few clear-cut chances being created. The breakthrough came through in the second period and predictably perhaps, it came from a defensive mistake when United 'keeper Kingsley attempted to stop a misplaced back-pass going out of play, but was dispossessed by Crawford who promptly crossed for McLatchie to loft the ball into the net.

The Wearside contingent in the crowd went wild with delight and moments later McLatchie almost added a second, only to be barged off the ball as he was about to score. The home side then pressed forward looking desperately for an equaliser, but the Sunderland defence held firm to record their first-ever league victory over their arch-rivals.

NEWCASTLE UNITED 2
McFARLANE A.GARDNER

SUNDERLAND 4
R.HOGG (3) BECKTON

DATE: 23 December 1899
VENUE: St. James' Park
ATTENDANCE: 21,000
COMPETITION: League Division One
REFEREE: Mr. J. Fox

NEWCASTLE UTD: Kingsley, Lindsay, D.Gardner, Aitken, Higgins, Carr, Rogers, Stevenson, A.Gardner, McFarlane, Fraser.

SUNDERLAND: Doig, McCombie, McNeil, Ferguson, McAllister, Raisbeck, W.Hogg, Leslie, R.Hogg, Beckton, McLatchie.

Sunderland's final game of the nineteenth century saw them claim a resounding victory over the Magpies with their centre-forward Bobby Hogg finding the target three times to become the first player to register a hat-trick in North East football's most fiercely contested fixture.

The game however, was not as one-sided as the score-line suggests with the home side dominating the first 45 minutes and deservedly going in at the break with a 2-1 advantage. After Bobby Hogg had given Sunderland an early lead with a superb strike from the edge of the box, the home side took control with Doig in the Sunderland goal performing heroics to keep them at bay, before McFarland slotted home the equaliser after a poor back-pass by Ferguson had been intercepted. Then, three minutes before the break, Newcastle went in front when Rogers centred for Gardner who gave Doig no chance heading home from close-range.

The turning point in the game came early in the second half when a right-wing cross from Rogers appeared to be drifting out of play and Kingsley in the Newcastle goal inexplicably tried to palm the ball clear, only to present Bobby Hogg with the easiest of chances to level the scores. Thereafter, there was only one team in the contest as Sunderland stormed forward and with the home defence in total disarray, they netted two further goals in the six minutes that followed their equaliser. Firstly, Beckton volleyed home after a sweeping passing move and then Bobby Hogg completed his hat-trick, heading home McLatchie's cross in great style.

Sunderland's second-half performance had been an outstanding display of fast, attacking football and they thoroughly deserved their victory, while Newcastle were left to reflect on what might have been, having been totally in control of the contest at the break.

5

BILLY HOGG

NEWCASTLE UNITED 0
SUNDERLAND 2
W.HOGG (25) R.HOGG (70)

DATE: 24 April 1901
VENUE: St. James' Park
ATTENDANCE: 18,594
COMPETITION: League Division One
REFEREE: Mr. Stott

NEWCASTLE UTD: Kingsley, Burgess, D.Gardner, Ghee, Aitken, Carr, A.Gardner, Niblo, Peddie, Heywood, Fraser.

SUNDERLAND: Doig, McCombie, Watson, Ferguson, McAllister, Jackson, W.Hogg, R.Hogg, Millar, Livingstone, McLatchie.

This Tyne-Wear derby was a rearranged fixture after the original Good Friday game had been postponed two hours before kick-off due to unprecedented crowd scenes at St. James' Park. In order to ensure there would be no repetition, there was a strong police presence throughout Newcastle in the hours leading up to the game and particularly at St. James' Park. Officers were stationed at regular intervals around the ground with mounted police guarding the perimeter fence, which had been scaled by countless thousands during the Good Friday incident.

The operation proved to be a complete success with no incidents reported as 18,500 fans packed the ground for the eagerly awaited encounter. For Sunderland, it was their final game of the season and they were still in with a great chance of winning the title, whereas Newcastle, who had been in contention for most of the campaign, were sitting in sixth place and very much out of the race.

Newcastle started brightly enough and a mistake by Watson gave them a great chance in the opening minutes, but a brilliant last-ditch tackle by McCrombie saved the day for the visitors. United came closer still soon afterwards when Heywood set up a great chance for Peddie, but the United forward's shot was well wide. Gradually however, Sunderland began to take control of the game and it came as no surprise when they took the lead after 25 minutes. A fine move saw Millar sent clear and when his shot was parried by Kingsley, Billy Hogg was on hand to slot home the rebound. Newcastle started the second half brightly and were desperately unlucky not to equalise when a tremendous shot from Peddie struck the bar. The game then developed into an end-to-end encounter with Sunderland gradually beginning to look more dangerous with their fast, attacking wing play and only desperate goalkeeping from Kingsley kept the visitors at bay. The respite was short-lived however, when a weak clearance from Burgess presented Bobby Hogg with a chance and even though the angle was difficult, he beat Kingsley with a terrific cross shot. Thereafter, Sunderland took control and were happy to play possession football and see the game out until the final whistle. It was a great victory for Sunderland and it put them on top of the league ahead of Liverpool on goal difference, but their hopes of another title were dashed a few days later when the Merseysiders secured a narrow 1-0 victory over West Bromwich Albion in their final game, to pip them at the post.

NEWCASTLE UNITED 0
SUNDERLAND 1
GEMMELL (26)

DATE: 28 September 1901
VENUE: St. James' Park
ATTENDANCE: 23,330
COMPETITION: League Division One
REFEREE: Mr. Lewis

NEWCASTLE UTD: Kingsley, D.Gardner, Davidson, Ghee, Aitken, Carr, A.Gardner, McFarlane, Niblo, Orr, Roberts.

SUNDERLAND: Doig, McCombie, Watson, Ferguson, McAllister, Jackson, W.Hogg, R.Hogg, Millar, Gemmell, McLatchie.

Yet again there was a strong police presence around St. James' Park and as a precaution to ensure supporters were able to watch the game in comfort, the gates were closed 30 minutes before kick-off, hence the relatively disappointing attendance of less than 25,000. The conditions were perfect, a beautiful sunny day and perhaps too hot for football, as United kicked-off attacking down the slope.

The home side were soon enjoying the better of the early exchanges with Niblo going close with a dipping shot which just cleared the bar. Then Billy Hogg broke through for the visitors, only to be thwarted by Kingsley who raced from his line to save at the Sunderland forward's feet. United were enjoying the lion's share of possession though and should have gone in front when Niblo shot hopelessly wide from a great position. Against the run of play, Sunderland took the lead with a somewhat fortuitous goal when Gemmell, 30 yards out, floated a hopeful high ball into the box. There seemed to be no danger, but to the amazement of spectators and players alike, the ball curled over Kingsley in the Newcastle goal and into the net. It was a bad mistake by the United 'keeper who seemed to have completely misjudged the flight of the ball.

Encouraged by their good fortune, SAFC surged forward looking to increase their lead and after a long-range effort from McLatchie had sailed wide, Bobby Hogg came close with a terrific shot that brought an excellent save from Kingsley. As the first half came to a close, United rallied and came close when only a brilliant save by Doig prevented Aitken from levelling the scores.

Sunderland attacked from the restart and McLatchie sent a shot just past the upright, then only a superb diving save from Kingsley prevented Bill Hogg from increasing the visitors' lead. United were struggling to get back into the game at this stage and their task became even greater when Gardner, who had been limping badly, was forced to go off. The United full-back was off the park for seven minutes during which Sunderland should have increased their lead following a flowing move that ended with Billy Hogg firing a cross-shot past Kingsley only for Gemmell to inexplicably help the ball over the line with his hand. It was an incredible error of judgement by the Sunderland forward and it cost his side a priceless second goal that would have made the game safe. Instead, their supporters were forced to endure the remaining minutes with the game on a knife edge as the home side searched for an equaliser, although with the Sunderland defence showing great form they were unable to create a single opening.

The victory was one of the highlights of a great season for Sunderland that saw them lift their fourth league title with long-serving stars Ted Doig and Jimmy Millar picking up their fourth League Championship medals.

JIMMY GEMMELL

DICKY JACKSON

DATE: 26 December 1903
VENUE: St. James' Park
ATTENDANCE: 28,797
COMPETITION: League Division One
REFEREE: Mr. J. Lewis

NEWCASTLE UTD: Kingsley, Tildesley, Willis, Gardner, Veitch, Aitken, Turner, Rutherford, Appleyard, McColl, Templeton.

SUNDERLAND: Doig, McCombie, Watson, Farquhar, McAllister, Jackson, Craggs, Bridgett, Hogg, Gemmell, Buckle.

Having beaten Sunderland for the first time at St. James' Park the previous season, hopes of a repeat performance were high among United fans, but on the day, their team had no answer to a brilliant Sunderland side that dominated the game from the start and ran out comfortable winners.

There was cause for concern before the game when it became apparent that Mr. Lewis, the referee, had missed his train connection from Blackburn. The game was not delayed however as both clubs agreed that one of the linesmen, Mr. Dennis of Middlesbrough, should take charge until the arrival of Mr. Lewis who turned up 20 minutes late.

Heavy rain in the days leading up to the game meant the conditions were difficult as Appleyard kicked off for Newcastle towards the Town goal and against a stiff breeze. Sunderland had been staying at Seaton Carew for special training and their energy and enthusiasm was certainly apparent as they tore into the home side from the start. The home side were weathering the storm extremely well until disaster struck when Willis hesitated when trying to clear, allowing Bridgett to steal up and win possession before firing the ball past Kingsley in the Newcastle goal.

Newcastle responded bravely and Appleyard almost equalised, but a moment or two later, Sunderland were 2-0 up after Bridgett scored a brilliant solo-goal. Although Newcastle came back strongly towards the end of the half and came close on a couple of occasions, it was the visitors who were very much in control as the half-time whistle blew.

There were few goalscoring opportunities in the second period which was totally dominated by Sunderland, but United were given a lifeline with five minutes remaining when Rutherford pulled a goal back. Moments later, Vietch almost netted the equaliser, but any hopes of United pulling the game out of the fire were dashed in the final minute when Sunderland broke quickly and Buckle netted the third.

NEWCASTLE UNITED 1
RUTHERFORD (85)

SUNDERLAND 3
BRIDGETT (20, 23) BUCKLE (89)

SUNDERLAND 3
JACKSON (1, 62) BUCKLE (30)

NEWCASTLE UNITED 1
McWILLIAM (29)

DATE: 24 December 1904
VENUE: Roker Park
ATTENDANCE: 34,000
COMPETITION: League Division One
REFEREE: Mr. Kirkham

SUNDERLAND: Webb, Rhodes, Watson, Farquhar, Fullarton, Jackson, Hogg, Bridgett, Common, Gemmell, Buckle.

NEWCASTLE UTD: Lawrence, McCombie, Carr, Gardner, Veitch, McWilliam, Rutherford, Howie, Appleyard, Orr, Gosnell.

Sunderland gave their supporters an early Christmas present with a resounding victory over the Magpies, their first-ever success over their arch-rivals on home territory. Newcastle were strong favourites having been in superb form in the weeks leading up to the game and were sitting proudly at the top of the table, but on the day, they were no match for a rampant Sunderland side who got off to the most explosive of starts.

Gardner won the toss and decided to attack the Fulwell End, but straight from the kick-off Sunderland attacked down the right and Bridgett was immediately brought down by Carr. When Rhodes floated in the resultant free-kick, Jackson beat McCrombie to the ball to head home and give Sunderland the lead with only 30 seconds on the clock!

The goal stunned United and buoyed by their early success, Sunderland surged forward with the visitors' defence struggling to cope with their sustained attacking play. The Magpies were hanging on desperately, but after 29 minutes and totally against the run of play, they managed to snatch an equaliser with the most fortuitous of goals. McWilliam attempted the most ambitious of long-range shots from the Main Stand touchline which Webb in the Sunderland goal appeared to have covered, only to allow the ball to slip from his grasp and roll agonisingly over the line.

The goal was a blow to the home side who had dominated the game up to that point, but within a minute they regained the lead. A great ball by Buckle sent Hogg racing towards goal to fire in a terrific shot which Lawrence couldn't hold and Buckle picked up the rebound to fire home.

Amazingly, straight from the restart, United were presented a great chance to level the scores when a great ball from Howie sent Rutherford into the penalty area where he was brought crashing to the ground after a thunderous challenge by Watson. The referee had no hesitation in awarding a penalty-kick, but when Appleyard stepped up, he fired his shot yards wide of the upright.

The second half began with Newcastle trying desperately to get back into the game, but their forwards were having little joy against a resolute Sunderland defence and soon the home side took control with wave after wave of attacks on the visitors goal where Lawrence and his defenders were performing heroics to keep them at bay.

Then on 62 minutes, Sunderland won a corner and when the ball was floated in, United won possession, but instead of clearing their lines, Vietch and Orr attempted to play their way out of trouble allowing Jackson to step in and fire the ball home. After that, it was all Sunderland with Lawrence making a number of outstanding saves to keep the marauding Sunderland forwards out and at the final whistle, the home side were comfortable winners.

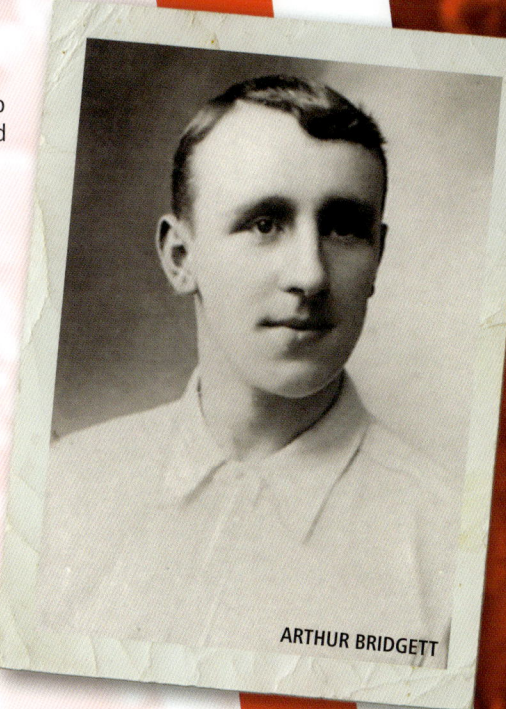

ARTHUR BRIDGETT

GEORGE HOLLEY

DATE: 22 April 1905
VENUE: St. James' Park
ATTENDANCE: 28,497
COMPETITION: League Division One
REFEREE: Mr. F. Kirkham

NEWCASTLE UTD: Lawrence, McCombie, Carr, Gardner, Aitken, McWilliam, Rutherford, Howie, Appleyard, Veitch, Gosnell.

SUNDERLAND: Webb, Rhodes, Watson, Willis, Barrie, Jackson, Hogg, Holley, Gemmell, Bridgett, Buckle.

The stakes could hardly have been higher as the two sides ran out in front of a capacity St. James' Park crowd for this end-of-season encounter, particularly for Newcastle who were within touching distance of their first-ever First Division title.

In the week leading up to the game, rumours were circulating on Tyneside that Sunderland might be persuaded to 'take it easy', but those responsible were soon made to eat their words as the visitors produced an outstanding display to record a truly memorable victory.

Predictably, there was a massive interest in the game and once again there were crowd problems prior to kick-off with countless thousands locked out and quite a number scaling the perimeter walls to gain entry prompting fears of a repetition of the Good Friday events a few years earlier. Severe rainstorms had swept across Tyneside in the hours leading up to the game and the heavy conditions were certainly less than perfect as United kicked-off attacking the Leazes End.

Sunderland took the game to United from the start with the home side struggling to come to terms with their opponents' heavy tackling; Watson in particular was certainly taking no prisoners! The first clear-cut chance came following a flowing Sunderland move which culminated in Bridgett firing in a goal-bound effort that Lawrence was perhaps somewhat fortunate to keep out. Soon afterwards, after 20 minutes play, Sunderland took the lead when United struggled to clear from a corner and after a series of shots were charged down, Carr attempted to shepherd the ball out of play only to be dispossessed by Holley. The Sunderland forward cut in on goal and although his shot was straight at Lawrence, the United 'keeper somehow allowed the ball to slip through his legs and into the net.

Five minutes later, the game swung strongly in Sunderland's favour when United were reduced to ten men following an injury to Gardner and almost immediately the visitor's doubled their advantage. United's defence were struggling to deal with the pace of the Sunderland forwards and Buckle was able to weave his way past

NEWCASTLE UNITED 1
VIETCH (35 PEN)

SUNDERLAND 3
HOLLEY (20, 83) BUCKLE (26)

McCombie and Vietch to finish with a rising drive into the roof of the net. United then came back strongly and after Appleyard had a goal disallowed for offside, they were awarded a penalty when the same player was fouled inside the box by Rhodes. Vietch was entrusted with the kick and he duly obliged firing home low to the 'keeper's left and just inside the post.

After half time the ten men of United put up a brave show, but were generally restricted to long-range efforts which were dealt with easily by Webb in the Sunderland goal. The home side did come close on a couple of occasions however, with Rutherford missing a great opportunity after Gosnell had whipped the ball across the box, but other than that the Sunderland defence held firm. The game was finally put beyond Newcastle seven minutes from time when Gemmell passed the ball through to Holley who fired home from what appeared to be an offside position. Despite United's protests, the goal was allowed to stand to bring an end to a wretched afternoon for the home side. The defeat was a big blow to Magpie supporters, but their spirits were lifted soon afterwards when their team clinched the title, finishing one point ahead of second-placed Everton.

SUNDERLAND 3
BRIDGETT (3, 48) GEMMELL (65)

NEWCASTLE UNITED 2
HOWIE (14) ORR (66)

DATE: 2 September 1905
VENUE: Roker Park
ATTENDANCE: 30,000
COMPETITION: League Division One
REFEREE: Mr. G. Copes

SUNDERLAND: Naisby, Rhodes, Watson, Farquhar, Barrie, Willis, Hogg, Holley, Gemmell, Bridgett, Buckle.

NEWCASTLE UTD: Lawrence, McCombie, Carr, Gardner, Aitken, Vietch, Rutherford, Howie, Hardinge, Orr, Gosnall.

Tyne-Wear derby matches are always the most eagerly awaited fixture on the North East football calendar, but with United having clinched the league championship the previous campaign, this match at Roker Park on the opening day of the new season certainly gave SAFC an added incentive to put one over on their arch-rivals.

A capacity 30,000 crowd saw Aitken win the toss for the visitors and elect to play with the strong westerly wind that was blowing through Roker Park. Sunderland could hardly have got off to a better start when they drew first blood with only three minutes on the clock. The goal was engineered by Holley, who opened the United defence with a superb pass to Bridgett who promptly fired home.

United responded immediately with a series of raids on the home goal and Naisby was forced to make a couple of crucial saves. After 15 minutes, the visitors got their reward when they won a free-kick 20 yards out and Naisby stepped up to power a low shot through the packed penalty area and into the net. Moments later, Rutherford had a great chance to give the visitors the lead, but fired wide with the goal at his mercy. Soon afterwards, the United forward did have the ball in the net, but his effort was disallowed by the referee. At this stage Newcastle were having the better of exchanges, but right on half-time Sunderland almost regained the lead when Lawrence fumbled a shot from Holley and only a last-ditch goal-line clearance by Carr spared the United 'keeper's blushes.

Sunderland began the second half very much in the ascendency and on 49 minutes they were rewarded when Bridgett netted their second with a low drive that gave Lawrence no chance. With their supporters now in full voice, the home side surged forward with a series of raids that had the Newcastle rear-guard defending desperately. Lawrence, in outstanding form, produced a series of brilliant saves to deny the Roker forwards, but on 65 minutes, he was given no chance when Gemmell netted the third goal with a terrific finish.

That looked to have made the game safe for Sunderland, but before the cheering had died down United had pulled a goal back when Orr scored from close-range. Thereafter, somewhat surprisingly, there was little threat on the Sunderland goal as Newcastle seemed to run out of attacking ideas and had it not been for Lawrence in the United goal, the home side could easily have increased their advantage.

SUNDERLAND 2
McINTOSH (77) HOLLEY (85)
NEWCASTLE UNITED 0

DATE: 20 March 1907
VENUE: Roker Park
ATTENDANCE: 35,000
COMPETITION: League Division One
REFEREE: Mr. T. P. Campbell

SUNDERLAND: Ward, Rhodes, Daykin, Tait, McGhie, McConnell, Raine, Hogg, McIntosh, Holley, Bridgett.

NEWCASTLE UTD: Kelsey, McCracken, McCombie, Gardner, Speedie, McWilliams, Rutherford, Howie, Appleyard, Brown, Gosnell.

League leaders Newcastle United were very much favourites for this eagerly awaited encounter having established themselves as odds-on favourites for the title. However, no fixture is a greater leveller than a local derby, with Sunderland fans desperate to knock their arch-rivals off their lofty perch!

There was a crowd of about 35,000 inside Roker Park on a bright, sunny afternoon as United kicked-off attacking the Fulwell End goal. Almost immediately, the home defence was put under pressure when they conceded a free-kick just outside the box and when McCracken floated the ball in, Appleyard came within a whisker of getting his head on the ball at the far post. The same player had another chance a few minutes later, but lifted his shot over the bar. Gradually however, Sunderland began to take control with the visitors' defence struggling to cope with the pace of their attack and they should have gone in front mid-way through the half when Bridgett missed a great chance. McIntosh created the opening with a great ball to send the Sunderland winger clean through on goal, but with only Kelsey to beat, he lifted the ball over the bar much to the annoyance of the home fans. At the break, the score-line was still blank, which was probably a fair reflection of the first 45 minutes during which neither side had dominated.

The game continued at a furious pace after the break, but with both defences in tremendous form, clear goalscoring opportunities were few and far between. Then on 70 minutes, United were presented with a great opportunity to draw first blood when Rutherford was brought down in the box by McConnell. McCracken stepped up to take the spot-kick, but much to the joy of the home supporters, the United full-back drove the ball well wide of the post.

The miss seemed to inspire Sunderland and roared on by their fanatical fans they began to lay siege on the visitors' goal. The breakthrough finally came 13 minutes from time when Raine crossed for Holley to send in a terrific shot which struck the underside of the bar and McIntosh was first to react to force the ball over the line.

Soon afterwards, United were reduced to ten men when McCracken limped off and with only five minutes remaining, Sunderland put the game beyond doubt with a flowing move that culminated in Holley firing home from close range.

SUNDERLAND AFC 1906-07
BACK: TAIT, McGHIE, RHODES, WARD, WATSON, McCONNELL, DAYKIN.
FRONT: HOGG, McINTOSH, GEMMELL, HALL, BRIDGETT.

NEWCASTLE UNITED 1
HOWIE (85)
SUNDERLAND 3
HOLLEY (40) LOW (57) BRIDGETT (65)

DATE: 18 April 1908
VENUE: St. James' Park
ATTENDANCE: 50,000
COMPETITION: League Division One

NEWCASTLE UTD: Lawrence, McCombie, Carr, Gardner, Veitch, Willis, Duncan, Howie, Appleyard, Speedie, Gosnell.

SUNDERLAND: Roose, Marples, Foster, Tait, Low, Jarvie, McIntosh, Hogg, Raybould, Holley, Bridgett.

Sunderland dominated this encounter from the off and gained a well-deserved victory against their arch-rivals in what turned out to be a one-sided game at St. James' Park. The visitors were in control throughout with United's poor overall performance possibly suggesting that one or two of their players had their eyes on the forthcoming FA Cup final against Wolverhampton Wanderers at Crystal Palace a week later.

Newcastle won the toss and decided to play with the strong wind that was blowing down the pitch, although they soon became aware that this gave them little advantage as Sunderland took control with some fine attacking play. Holley was the main thorn in the side of the home defence and it was perhaps fitting that he should give the visitors the lead five minutes before the break when he surged past McCombie to finish in style.

Sunderland doubled their advantage soon after the break when McCombie headed clear only for Low to fire home a stunning volley from outside the box that gave Lawrence in the United goal no chance. A third goal came soon afterwards when Bridgett took on the United defence with a brilliant run down the wing before cutting in to unleash a terrific shot that fairly screamed into the net. It was a brilliant solo-effort and typical of the England international who, on his day, had few peers in the top-class game. After that, Sunderland were content to play possession football and while Howie did manage to pull a goal back for the home side, the result was never in doubt and Sunderland were unfortunate not to have added a fourth goal when Raybould netted only to see his effort ruled out for offside.

The result ensured Sunderland's safety in Division One after what had been a disappointing campaign that saw them flirting with relegation throughout. As for Newcastle, they would suffer an even greater disappointment a week later when they were beaten 3-1 by Wolves in the FA Cup final.

HARRY LOW

NEWCASTLE UNITED 1
SHEPHERD (43 PEN)

SUNDERLAND 9
HOGG (8, 58, 77) HOLLEY (47, 62, 67)
BRIDGETT (69, 71) MORDUE (73)

DATE: 5 December 1908
VENUE: St. James' Park
ATTENDANCE: 56,000
COMPETITION: League Division One
REFEREE: Mr. A. E. Farrant

NEWCASTLE UTD: Lawrence, Whitsun, Pudan, Liddell, Veitch, Willis, Duncan, Higgins, Shepherd, Wilson, Gosnell.

SUNDERLAND: Roose, Foster, Milton, Daykin, Thomson, Low, Mordue, Hogg, Brown, Holley, Bridgett.

Without doubt, this was the most remarkable Sunderland victory in the long history of Tyne-Wear derbies and one which it is almost certain, will never be equalled. To say that Newcastle United were annihilated doesn't really do justice to an incredible second-half performance by Sunderland that saw them find the net no fewer than eight times in twenty-six unbelievable minutes.

It was a result that sent shockwaves through the English game particularly bearing in mind that the Magpies were enjoying a rich vein of form going into the game and would eventually go on to lift the League Championship at the end of the campaign. But in that amazing second half at St. James' Park, the home side were completely destroyed by a display of attacking football the like of which has never been witnessed in a Tyne-Wear derby, either before or since and one that would live long in the memory for both sets of supporters although for vastly differing reasons. Even now, the scoreline remains a record for an away victory in English football's top division and if ever Sunderland fans enjoyed the 'Bragging Rights' of Tyne-Wear derbies, then it was on this truly unbelievable afternoon in December 1908.

Given the final score, it's hard to imagine that the first-half was a fairly even encounter and United could have actually drawn first blood after only six minutes when Duncan fired over from a great position. Soon afterwards however, Sunderland took the lead with their first attack of the game. Mordue engineered the goal when he beat Pudan out on the right and then rounded Lawrence in the United goal before presenting Hogg with the easiest of chances to send the Sunderland contingent in the crowd wild with delight.

It was soon apparent that man for man, the visitors enjoyed a significant physical advantage with Charlie Thomson in particular taking no prisoners, before eventually being cautioned by the referee after dumping Shepherd onto the ash track with a thunderous challenge. United weren't holding back though and soon afterwards Daykin was knocked unconscious with a blow to the face which needed lengthy treatment before he could return to the fray.

Just before half-time United drew level with a hotly disputed penalty after Thomson was adjudged to have handled in the box. After lengthy protests by the Sunderland players, the referee consulted both linesmen, but still awarded the spot-kick which was duly despatched by Shepherd.

The second period began with Sunderland on the attack and on 48 minutes they regained the lead following a brilliant run by Bridgett whose cross was only partially cleared by the United defence allowing Hogg to fire the ball high into the net. Even at this stage there was no hint of the avalanche of goals that was about to end up in the home side's net, but after Hogg stole in to net the third ten minutes later, the United defence seemed to completely crumble. On 63 minutes Holley netted the fourth following a brilliant dribble through the static home rearguard and four minutes later he completed his hat-trick when he smashed Mordue's cross past the helpless Lawrence. Then Bridgett got in on the act with two long-range efforts before Mordue added the eighth with a low shot into the corner of the net. Finally, on 76 minutes Hogg completed his hat-trick to bring to an end a thoroughly miserable afternoon for the Magpies and their supporters.

Back on Wearside, there were great celebrations as the news of the game filtered through, particularly at Roker Park where fans watching a reserve match looked on in amazement at the constantly changing scoreboard with many thinking they were victims of a cruel hoax! In town, crowds gathered outside the Echo offices in Bridge Street and there was a huge roar when the final score was announced, followed by scenes of joy the like of which had never been witnessed previously.

A few days after the game, a parcel arrived at Roker Park marked for the attention of Sunderland manager Bob Kyle.

To his surprise, when he opened the package he found two dead magpies together with a note from a delighted supporter in Consett congratulating him on his team's great victory!

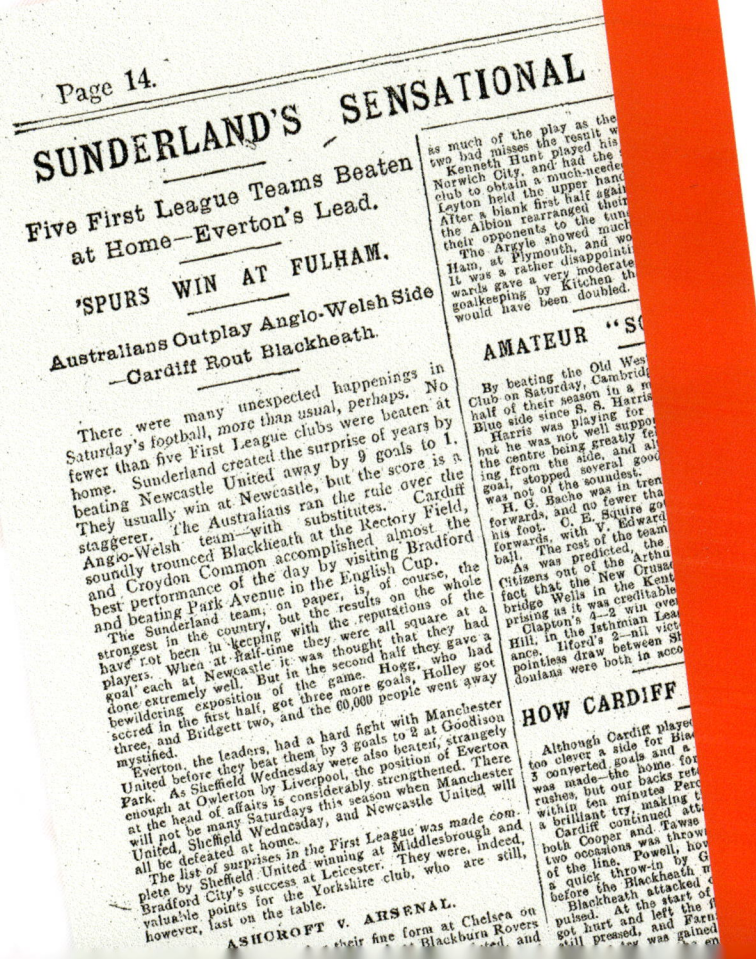

SUNDERLAND 3
BROWN (47, 50) HOLLEY (75)

NEWCASTLE UNITED 1
SHEPHERD (1)

DATE: 10 April 1909
VENUE: Roker Park
ATTENDANCE: 40,000
COMPETITION: League Division One
REFEREE: Mr. Hammond

SUNDERLAND: Roose, Foster, Milton, Tait, Thomson, Jarvie, Mordue, Low, Brown, Holley, Bridgett.

NEWCASTLE UTD: Lawrence, McCracken, Whitsun, Howie, Veitch, McWilliam, Rutherford, Stewart, Shepherd, Wilson, Anderson.

If Newcastle supporters thought that the return fixture at Roker Park would bring immediate revenge for the 9-1 drubbing at St. James' Park a few months earlier, then they were sadly mistaken. Nevertheless, they did produce a much more competitive performance and actually took the lead with less than a minute on the clock.

Sunderland started the game attacking the Fulwell End, but the visitors quickly gained possession and when McWilliam crossed, Shepherd beat Jarvie and Thomson before firing home past Roose to stun the home crowd. It was a brilliant finish, but one that came at a great cost to the visitors when the United centre-forward was injured as he fired the ball home and was carried off immediately afterwards. After lengthy treatment, he did manage to return to the action, but was clearly struggling throughout the first period and was unable to carry on after the half-time break.

With United now down to ten men, Sunderland immediately took advantage when Brown levelled the scores two minutes into the half with a brilliant shot following a poor clearance from McCracken. Three minutes later, the home side were in front and again it was Brown who was on target, forcing the ball home following a scramble in front of the United goal. Without Shepherd leading their attack, Newcastle offered little threat and with 15 minutes remaining

ARTHUR BROWN

Sunderland made the game safe when Brown took on the United defence only to be brought down as he was about to shoot. Holley stepped up to take the kick and while Lawrence saved his first shot, the Sunderland winger followed up to net the rebound. Soon afterwards Brown had the ball in the net again only to be denied his hat-trick when the goal was ruled out for offside.

SUNDERLAND 2
MORDUE (32) COLEMAN (86)

NEWCASTLE UNITED 1
SHEPHERD (PEN 80)

DATE: 1 September 1910
VENUE: Roker Park
ATTENDANCE: 29,000
COMPETITION: League Division One
REFEREE: Mr. T. P. Campbell

SUNDERLAND: Roose, Troughear, Milton, Tait, Thomson, Low, Mordue, Coleman, Holley, Gemmell, Bridgett.

NEWCASTLE UTD: Lawrence, McCracken, Whitson, Veitch, Low, McWilliam, Rutherford, Stewart, Shepherd, Higgin, Wilson.

The opening game of the season could not have provided a bigger attraction on Wearside and while the scoreline suggests a closely fought encounter, Sunderland were much the stronger side throughout and finished the game as worthy winners.

From the start, the home side enjoyed the better of exchanges with Mordue in particular proving to be something of a handful for the United defence with his powerful runs and fierce shooting. In fact, on one occasion the Sunderland winger hit the ball with such power that it burst through the side-netting and ended up in the goal behind the stunned United 'keeper and the game was held up for some minutes while the necessary repairs were carried out.

Sunderland deservedly took the lead on 32 minutes when Mordue fired home after Lawrence had parried a terrific shot from Coleman and then Bridgett came close to adding a second, only to be foiled by the United 'keeper. Sunderland maintained their advantage up to half-time, but after the break the visitors began to show a lot more aggression in their play as they went in search of the equaliser.

Nevertheless, it was the home side who were enjoying the lion's share of attacking play and only a superb save from Lawrence prevented Holley from doubling their advantage. Then Roose in the Sunderland goal denied the visitors an equaliser when he snatched the ball off Rutherford's toes as the United forward delayed his shot right in front of goal.

Whilst Sunderland still looked the more likely to score, their single goal advantage was always a precarious one and it perhaps came as no surprise when United snatched an equaliser with only ten minutes remaining. The goal came following a scramble in front of the Sunderland goal when Troughear was adjudged to have handled, although referee Campbell needed to consult his linesman before awarding a penalty-kick which Shepherd duly converted.

Sunderland appeared to have let the game slip from their grasp but with only four minutes remaining they grabbed a dramatic winner when Coleman leapt to head home a corner and send the home fans wild with delight.

JACKIE MORDUE

SUNDERLAND 2
HOLLEY (35, 86)
NEWCASTLE UNITED 0

DATE: 28 December 1912
VENUE: Roker Park
ATTENDANCE: 30,000
COMPETITION: League Division One
REFEREE: Mr. J. T. Howcroft

SUNDERLAND: Butler, Gladwin, Milton, Cuggy, Thomson, Low, Mordue, Buchan, Richardson, Holley, Martin.

NEWCASTLE UTD: Lawrence, McCracken, Little, Hewison, Low, Hay, Duncan, McTavish, Higgins, Wilson, Hibbert.

While George Holley scored the vital goals in this comfortable victory for Sunderland, there was no doubt that Charlie Buchan was the star man for the home team. The Sunderland inside-right produced an almost flawless performance which surely must have impressed the England selectors sitting in the stands.

Buchan and his right-wing partner Jackie Mordue ran the United defence ragged for most of the game and at the end of the day Sunderland's margin of victory could have been much greater.

Newcastle did have their moments however, particularly in the early stages when they threatened to take the lead on more that one occasion, but it was Sunderland who made the vital breakthrough when Holley netted ten minutes before the break. Lawrence had parried a shot from Mordue and McCracken looked to have cleared the danger only for Holley to intercept and drive the ball into the net.

After the break Sunderland were very much in control with Buchan continuing to orchestrate proceedings in the middle of the park. United were still in the game though and it wasn't until the closing minutes that Sunderland finally made the game safe when Holley netted his second of the afternoon. The move began with Thomson winning possession in his own half before sending Richardson on a powerful run and as the United defence retreated, he slipped the ball through to Holley who finished the flowing move in style.

CHARLIE BUCHAN

The 1912-13 season was arguably the most successful in Sunderland's entire history as the club clinched their fifth league title and also came within a whisker of becoming the first team in the twentieth century to clinch the coveted League and FA Cup double.

In the cup, they had beaten Clapton Orient, Manchester City and Swindon Town before the sixth round draw set up a mouth-watering tie against their arch-rivals from Tyneside. Not surprisingly, the tie created huge interest in the North East and it would eventually take three games to settle the issue.

SUNDERLAND 0

NEWCASTLE UNITED 0

DATE: 8 March 1913
VENUE: Roker Park
ATTENDANCE: 28,720
COMPETITION: FA Cup Sixth Round
REFEREE: Mr. H. H. Taylor

SUNDERLAND: Butler, Gladwin, Milton, Cuggy, Thomson, Low, Mordue, Buchan, Richardson, Holley, Martin.

NEWCASTLE UTD: Lawrence, McCracken, Hudspeth, Veitch, Low, Hay, Rutherford, Stewart, Hibbert, Wilson, McDonald.

Sunderland went into the tie as strong favourites, but form soon went out of the window as Newcastle produced a solid performance to force a 0-0 draw in what turned out to be a somewhat disappointing encounter. The official attendance was given as 28,720 which was below Roker Park's capacity and probably due to the fact that Sunderland had controversially doubled the admission charges.

United's star centre-forward Albert Shepherd was forced to watch the game from the stands through injury which perhaps explains why the visitors posed only the occasional threat to the home goal. Nevertheless, fine defending by Newcastle saw the threat of Buchan, Mordue and Cuggy effectively nullified for long periods with only the occasional chance being created by the home side. The best of these fell to Mordue late in the game, but the winger volleyed over the bar from a great position inside the box.

After the game Sunderland captain Charlie Thomson agreed the game had been a disappointing affair: 'The game was not quite up to the quality of past encounters between Sunderland and Newcastle. The excitement was too great for the finer points of the game. On the whole I think United had slightly the best of it.'

SUNDERLAND AFC 1912-13

NEWCASTLE UNITED 2
McTAVISH (16) GLADWIN (88 OG)

SUNDERLAND 2
HOLLEY (28) BUCHAN (87)

DATE: 12 March 1913
VENUE: St. James' Park
ATTENDANCE: 56,717
COMPETITION: FA Cup Sixth Round Replay (AET)
REFEREE: Mr. J. Baker

NEWCASTLE UTD: Lawrence, McCracken, Hudspeth, Veitch, Low, Hay, McTavish, Hibbert, Shepherd, Wilson, McDonald.

SUNDERLAND: Butler, Gladwin, Milton, Cuggy, Thomson, Low, Mordue, Buchan, Richardson, Holley, Martin.

The replay created unprecedented interest and the gates were closed half an hour before kick-off with almost 57,000 packed inside the ground. Those fortunate enough to gain entry would witness a truly nail-biting, action-packed encounter that even after extra-time still failed to produce a winner.

With Shepherd returning to the United attack, hopes of a home win were high and they certainly had the better of the early exchanges before taking the lead after 16 minutes. Hibbert created the opening when he crossed from the right and when the Sunderland defence hesitated, McTavish was able to chest the ball over the line, much to the delight of the home supporters. Their joy was relatively short lived however, as Sunderland grabbed an equaliser soon afterwards when Holley was sent clear to beat Lawrence with a low shot.

After the break, Sunderland began to look the stronger side and they were desperately unlucky not to take the lead when Holley hit the post with a thunderous drive. Then, with only three minutes remaining, they looked to have won it when Buchan rose to head home from a corner, but straight from the kick-off, United grabbed the most fortuitous equaliser. Veitch tried his luck with a long speculative effort which Butler in the Sunderland goal appeared to have covered, but when Gladwin attempted to clear, he only succeeded in slicing the ball into his own net to level the tie. After half an hour of extra-time the sides could still not be separated.

Back on Wearside supporters were still bitterly disappointed at conceding the late equaliser and in his book 'A Lifetime in Football'

CHARLIE GLADWIN

Charlie Buchan recalled an incredible incident when the team returned home that night: 'On arrival at Sunderland, I boarded a tramcar with Gladwin. It was so full, we had to stand on the conductor's platform. There were two workmen standing beside us. One of them said to the other: "I wonder how much Gladwin got for putting the ball through his own goal." Without hesitation Gladwin hit the speaker on the chin. He toppled off the platform. The last I saw of him, was his feet waving in the air as he lay in the roadway!'

After the game, the Newcastle secretary had called correctly when a coin was tossed to determine which club would host the second replay and five days later, the teams ran out onto St. James' Park hoping to finally decide who would meet Burnley in the semi-final at Bramall Lane.

NEWCASTLE UNITED 0
SUNDERLAND 3
HOLLEY (8) MORDUE (40 PEN, 75)

DATE: 17 March 1913
VENUE: St. James' Park
ATTENDANCE: 25,000
COMPETITION: FA Cup Sixth Round Second Replay
REFEREE: Mr. Lewis

NEWCASTLE UTD: Lawrence, McCracken, Hudspeth, Veitch, Low, Hay, Duncan, McTavish, Hibbert, Stewart, Wilson.

SUNDERLAND: Butler, Gladwin, Milton, Cuggy, Thomson, Low, Mordue, Buchan, Richardson, Holley, Martin.

With several key players missing through injury, Newcastle were up against it from the start and although they had the backing of the majority of the crowd of just under 50,000, it was Sunderland who dominated the game. George Holley had been selected to play for England against Wales on the same day, but Sunderland successfully asked the FA for permission for their star forward to play in the cup-tie instead.

The game began with the home side facing a strong, icy cold wind and driving snow which became so severe at one point that many felt the referee should have abandoned the game. Sunderland were pretty much in control from the off and deservedly took the lead with only eight minutes on the clock, although there was a large slice of luck associated with the goal. Richardson crossed from the right and when Low volleyed goalwards, his effort rebounded off Holley and ballooned over Lawrence and into the net. Then five minutes before half-time, the game swung strongly in Sunderland's favour when Mordue netted from the spot after Martin had been pulled down by Vietch in the box.

The atrocious conditions eased somewhat after the break and Sunderland continued to dominate proceedings before finally putting the final nail in the Magpies' coffin with 15 minutes remaining. Again it was Mordue who was on target, this time with a terrific drive after a piece of brilliant attacking play by Buchan. At last the epic cup-tie was settled after no fewer than 134,245 supporters had watched the three games paying record aggregate receipts of £6,650.

In the semi-final Sunderland triumphed over Burnley after a yet another replay, but in the final at Crystal Palace they lost to a solitary Aston Villa goal. However, they did exact some revenge a few days after the final when they headed down to Villa Park where they secured a 1-1 draw to effectively pip their Midlands rivals to the league title.

BOBBY BEST

DATE: 25 December 1914
VENUE: St. James' Park
ATTENDANCE: 35,000
COMPETITION: League Division One
REFEREE: Mr. J. T. Howcroft

NEWCASTLE UTD: Lawrence, McCracken, Hudspeth, Hewison, Low, Hay, Douglas, King, Hibbert, Hall, Goodwin.

SUNDERLAND: Scott, Hobson, Ness, Cuggy, Thomson, Cringan, Mordue, Buchan, Best, Phillip, Martin.

Sunderland served up a huge helping of festive cheer for their supporters with this emphatic Christmas Day victory at St. James' Park and the game was also particularly memorable for centre-forward Bobby Best who netted a brilliant hat-trick.

The game was played in appalling conditions and the frozen pitch made it almost impossible to play good football, although Sunderland coped much better than their hosts and finished as comfortable winners.

Best gave Sunderland the lead after only eight minutes after fine play by Buchan, but United had a great chance to level the scores when Cringan brought down Douglas in the box. Hudspeth was United's regular penalty-taker and had only ever missed once from the spot previously, but on this occasion he drove his shot well wide.

Soon afterwards, Sunderland doubled their advantage with a brilliant solo goal by Best who received the ball from Mordue, and then left a string of United defenders in his wake before driving the ball past Lawrence in brilliant fashion. Then a minute before half-time Buchan won possession on the edge of the Newcastle box before driving home a terrific shot into the corner of the net.

The game was effectively over four minutes into the second half when hesitancy in the United defence allowed Best to steal in and complete his hat-trick and the Magpies' misery was complete on 70 minutes when Phillip netted the fifth. The home side did manage to pull back two goals, but even they were scored by Sunderland players, Scott and Ness each being credited with own-goals.

The following day, Newcastle gained ample revenge with a 4-2 victory in the return fixture at Roker Park and whilst no-one knew it at the time, this would be the last Tyne-Wear derby for almost five years due to the intervention of World War One.

NEWCASTLE UNITED 2
SCOTT (73 OG) NESS (75 OG)

SUNDERLAND 5
BEST (8, 31, 49) BUCHAN (44) PHILLIP (70)

SUNDERLAND 2

BUCHAN (17, 47)

NEWCASTLE UNITED 0

DATE: 22 November 1919
VENUE: Roker Park
ATTENDANCE: 47,148
COMPETITION: League Division One
REFEREE: Mr. L. N. Fletcher

SUNDERLAND: Allan, Hobson, Young, Cuggy, Kasher, Poole, Best, Buchan, Travers, Mordue, Martin.

NEWCASTLE UTD: Bradley, McCracken, Hudspeth, Curry, Low, Findlay, Robinson, Dixon, Hibbert, Booth, Ramsey.

The first derby match following the end of World War One created massive interest among both sets of supporters and huge crowds descended on Roker Park with an estimated 10,000 fans locked out when the gates were closed an hour before kick-off.

The attendance of 47,148 was a record for the ground and those fortunate enough to gain entry witnessed a resounding victory for Sunderland with newly-appointed captain Charlie Buchan grabbing the headlines with a 'man of the match' performance.

The Sunderland skipper was in outstanding form throughout and gave the home side the lead after 17 minutes when Martin took on the United defence before crossing from the left for Buchan to rise and plant a terrific header past the helpless Bradley. The United 'keeper soon afterwards saved brilliantly from Best and Buchan, but then the visitors missed a great opportunity to equalise when Robinson fired tamely across the face of goal after breaking through the Roker rearguard.

Sunderland took control of the game two minutes after the break when Buchan netted his second after being sent clear on the right by Best. The narrow angle meant the Sunderland skipper still had a lot to do, but he unleashed a tremendous shot that thundered low into the corner of the net. The Lads were then content to play possession football with Buchan enjoying the luxury of 'playing to the gallery' which angered Hudspeth who in the closing minutes, brought the Roker captain crashing to the ground with a brutal challenge. As Buchan was carried off the field, he received a tremendous reception.

NEWCASTLE UNITED 2
HIBBERT (18) ROBINSON (40)

SUNDERLAND 3
MORDUE (58) TRAVERS (75, 89)

DATE: 29 November 1919
VENUE: St. James' Park
ATTENDANCE: 63,000
COMPETITION: League Division One
REFEREE: Mr. L. N. Fletcher

NEWCASTLE UTD: Bradley, McCracken, Hudspeth, Curry, Low, Findlay, Robinson, Dixon, Hibbert, Hall, Ramsey.

SUNDERLAND: Allan, Hobson, Young, Cuggy, Kasher, Poole, Mordue, Buchan, Travers, Crossley, Martin.

Not for the first time in a Tyne-Wear derby, St. James' Park witnessed incredible crowd scenes in the streets surrounding the ground and the chaos continued long after the kick-off as supporters attempted to gain entry. The attendance of 63,000 was a record for the ground and the fans were treated to an excellent game that turned out to be something of a classic with great football and drama right through to the final whistle.

Even though the frozen pitch made conditions difficult, both sides produced some excellent football in a fairly even first half, although at the interval, United were very much in control having established a two-goal advantage. Hibbert gave Newcastle an early lead although there was some controversy surrounding the goal. Sunderland 'keeper Allan was in the process of attempting to clear when the United centre-forward appeared to kick the ball from his hands before slotting it into the empty net. Soon afterwards, Robinson doubled the home side's advantage and as the teams trooped off at the interval, Sunderland's prospects certainly looked bleak.

After the break, Newcastle seemed to be content to sit back and soak up the pressure, but the game turned when a defensive error allowed Sunderland back into the game. Martin put in a deep cross, but when Hibbert headed away, his weak clearance landed perfectly for Mordue to hammer home a terrific shot from the edge of the box. After that, it was all Sunderland and with 15 minutes to go, they grabbed an

BARNEY TRAVERS

equaliser when Travers latched onto Cuggy's pass before hitting home a first-time shot on the run. Then in the final minute, Martin sent Travers racing through the middle and after beating Hudspeth for pace, the Sunderland number nine drove home an unstoppable shot to snatch the most dramatic of winning goals. Moments later, the final whistle blew with the Sunderland contingent in the crowd going wild with delight while the massed ranks of United fans could only look on in utter disbelief.

SUNDERLAND 2
HAWES (47) PATERSON (57)
NEWCASTLE UNITED 0

DATE: 11 November 1922
VENUE: Roker Park
ATTENDANCE: 47,000
COMPETITION: League Division One
REFEREE: Mr. George Noel Watson

SUNDERLAND: Robson, Cresswell, England, Hunter, Parker, Poole, Donaldson, Buchan, Paterson, Hawes, Ellis.

NEWCASTLE UTD: Bradley, Hampson, Hudspeth, Curry, W.Low, Mooney, J.Low, Aitken, Harris, McDonald, Seymour.

Having failed to record a derby victory in their previous five attempts, this was certainly a welcome success for Sunderland, although it has to be said that they were somewhat fortuitous, having enjoyed the significant advantage of playing against ten men for more than half of the game.

The incident that turned the game came ten minutes before the break when Mooney was injured in an accidental collision with Hunter and was unable to take any further part in the game. Up until that point, the Newcastle left-half had done a pretty good man-marking job on Charlie Buchan, but as soon as he was relieved of Mooney's attentions, Sunderland's star inside-forward took control of the game.

The first period had been a fairly even encounter with both defences very much in control, but after the break the home side quickly dominated and took the lead on 47 minutes when Hawes rose to meet Donaldson's cross and leave Bradley helpless with a terrific header.

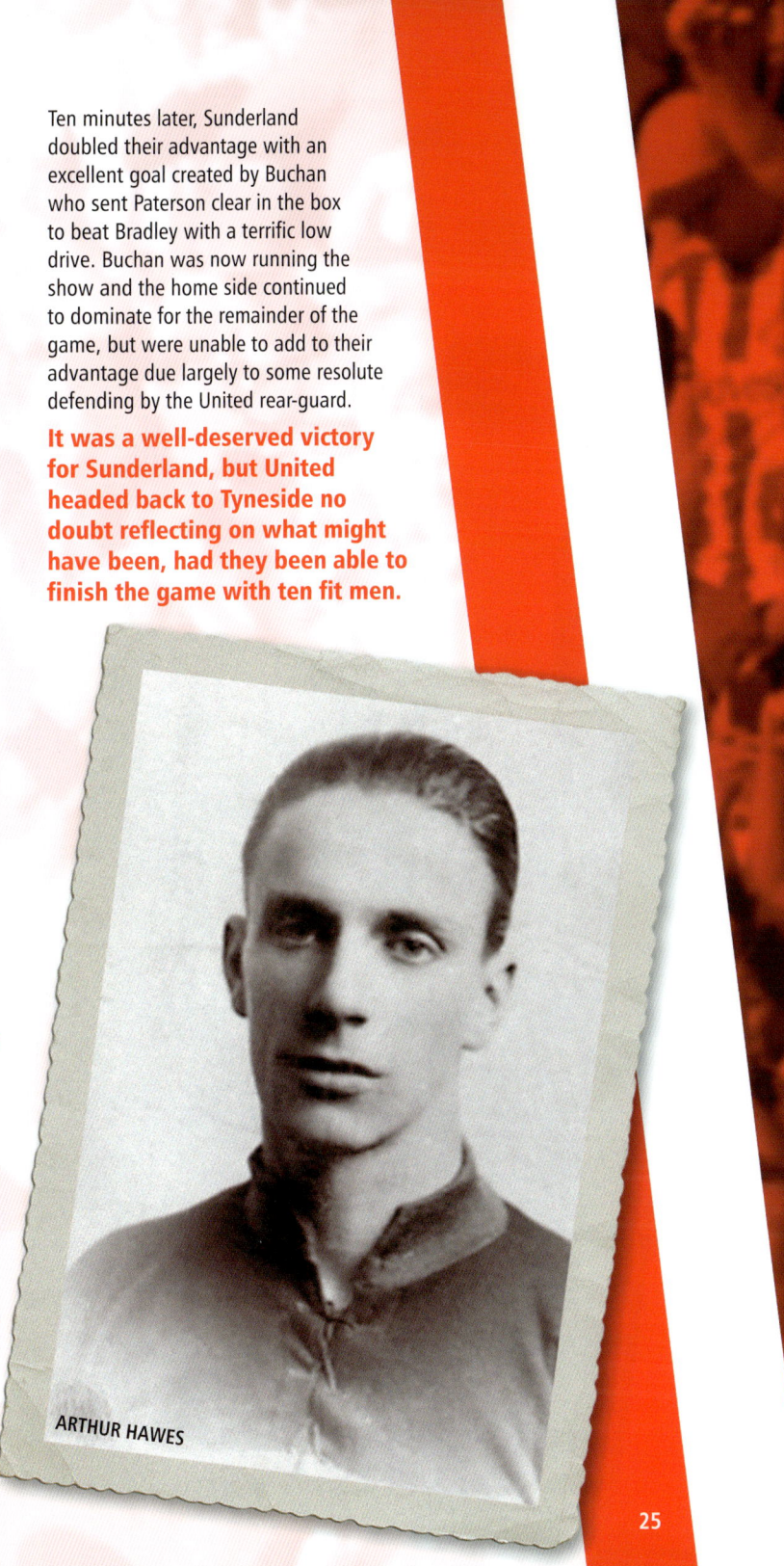

Ten minutes later, Sunderland doubled their advantage with an excellent goal created by Buchan who sent Paterson clear in the box to beat Bradley with a terrific low drive. Buchan was now running the show and the home side continued to dominate for the remainder of the game, but were unable to add to their advantage due largely to some resolute defending by the United rear-guard.

It was a well-deserved victory for Sunderland, but United headed back to Tyneside no doubt reflecting on what might have been, had they been able to finish the game with ten fit men.

ARTHUR HAWES

SUNDERLAND 3
PATERSON (19) HAWES (22, 23)

NEWCASTLE UNITED 2
HARRIS (6) SEYMOUR (36)

DATE: 15 December 1923
VENUE: Roker Park
ATTENDANCE: 45,000
COMPETITION: League Division One
REFEREE: Mr. Arthur Ward

SUNDERLAND: McInroy, Oakley, England, Clunas, Parker, Andrews, Grimshaw, Buchan, Paterson, Hawes, Ellis.

NEWCASTLE UTD: Bradley, Hampson, Hudspeth, Curry, Mooney, Gibson, Aitken, Cowan, Harris, McDonald, Seymour.

Most of the action in this five-goal thriller took place in the first 45 minutes, when at one point, Sunderland looked as though they were going to overwhelm United during a spell of truly breathtaking attacking football that saw them net three goals in four incredible minutes.

Indeed, at that point in the game many of the large contingent of Newcastle fans in the crowd must surely have had visions of another 9-1 drubbing! To their credit however, the Magpies managed to stem the flow before playing their way back into the game and were perhaps a little unfortunate to lose, particularly as they played the whole of the second half with their inside-right Cowan little more than a passenger following a first-half injury.

The visitors got off to a perfect start when Harris gave them the lead after only six minutes after playing a one-two with Seymour before lashing the ball high into the roof of the net. For a short period they seemed to be in control before Sunderland suddenly turned the game on its head in a devastating four-minute spell that saw them hit the target no fewer the three times.

Paterson opened the home side's account on 19 minutes when he forced the ball home after Grimshaw's shot had been stopped on the line. Three minutes later, Parker opened the United defence with a pin-point pass sending Hawes clear to beat Bradley with a low shot. Within a minute, it was three and again it was Hawes, this time heading home Grimshaw's cross with some style.

WARNEY CRESSWELL

For a while it looked as though Newcastle were about to crumble as wave after wave of Sunderland attacks rained down on their goal, but their defence held firm. Then with the half drawing to a close, the visitors broke clear to grab an unlikely second goal when Aitken raced through the Sunderland defence before passing to Seymour who gave McInroy no chance with a terrific shot. Moments later however, United's chances of getting back into the game took a severe blow when Cowan was carried off the field with a damaged knee. He did return after the break, but was very much a passenger out on the left-wing.

Not surprisingly, the second half failed to match the excitement of the first 45 minutes and while United did have a couple of opportunities to level the score, Sunderland were rarely in danger and finished the game as comfortable winners.

NEWCASTLE UNITED 0
SUNDERLAND 2
PATERSON (25, 71)

DATE: 22 December 1923
VENUE: St. James' Park
ATTENDANCE: 50,000
COMPETITION: League Division One
REFEREE: Mr. Lewis

NEWCASTLE UTD: Mutch, Hampson, Hudspeth, Curry, Low, Gibson, Aitken, Clarke, Harris, McDonald, Seymour.

SUNDERLAND: McInroy, Cresswell, England, Clunas, Parker, Andrews, Grimshaw, Buchan, Paterson, Hawes, Ellis.

Sunderland centre-forward Jock Paterson again proved to be something of a thorn in the side of the Magpies by finding the target for the third derby game in the row. This time, the Scot netted both goals in what turned out to be a hard-fought and perhaps slightly fortuitous victory for the visitors.

Newcastle enjoyed most of the early possession, without creating any real clear-cut openings due largely to some resolute play by the Sunderland defence. There had been little evidence of Buchan who had been closely marked from the start, but on 25 minutes, he managed to break clear and outpace Hudspeth before firing over a cross which Paterson headed home in great style. United came back strongly as the half drew to a close and were desperately close to an equaliser when Cresswell cleared off the line after McInroy had been beaten by Clarke's shot.

After the break Newcastle pressed forward in numbers, but were unable to find a way through the solid Sunderland rearguard where Cresswell and England in particular were in outstanding form. Sunderland were pretty much relying on breakaways at this stage of the game, but from one of these they were able to snatch a second goal when they capitalised on a mix-up in the United defence.

Mutch threw the ball out to Hampson which seemed to take the Newcastle full-back by surprise allowing Parker to gain possession before sending Hawes in on goal and when his shot was blocked, Paterson fired home the rebound.

The scoreline certainly flattered Sunderland and while United kept pressing and did hit the woodwork in the closing stages, they were unable to find their way back into the game.

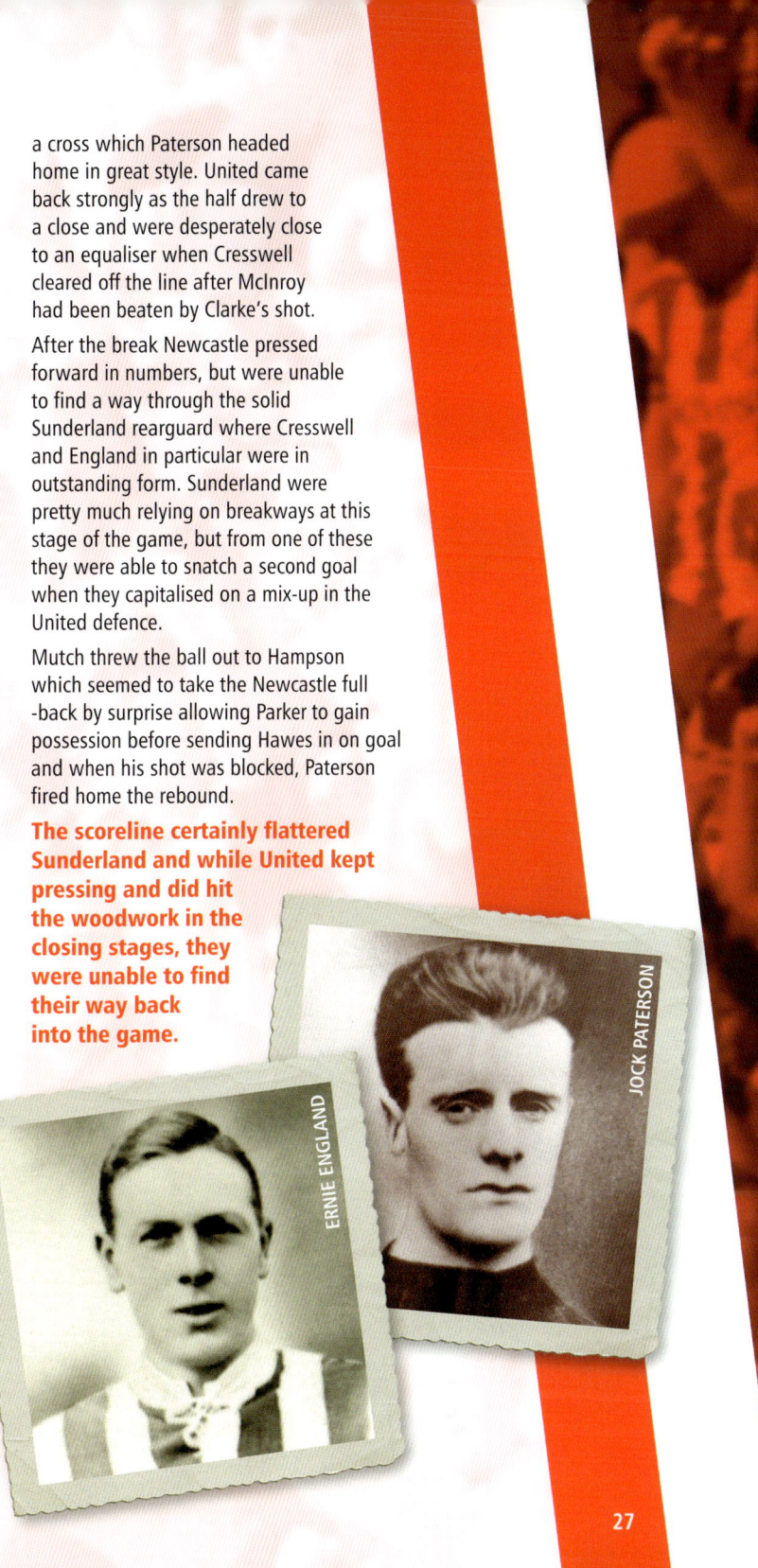

ERNIE ENGLAND

JOCK PATERSON

27

SUNDERLAND 2
HALLIDAY (25) DEATH (70)
NEWCASTLE UNITED 0

DATE: 30 October 1926
VENUE: Roker Park
ATTENDANCE: 31,152
COMPETITION: League Division One
REFEREE: Mr. Lewis

SUNDERLAND: McInroy, Cresswell, England, McGorian, Henderson, Andrews, Grimshaw, Kelly, Halliday, Gurney, Death.

NEWCASTLE UTD: Wilson, Maitland, Hudspeth, McKenzie, Spencer, Gibson, Urwin, Clarke, Loughlin, McDonald, Seymour.

Sunderland's victory in this closely-fought encounter was due largely to the brilliant form of goalkeeper Albert McInroy who kept the visitors at bay with a series of truly brilliant saves. United certainly enjoyed their fair share of the game and their fans were left to reflect on what might have been, had their star centre-forward Hughie Gallacher been able to play. Instead, the Scot was turning out for his country against Wales at Ibrox Park, scoring in a 3-0 victory.

However, in David Halliday Sunderland also had a Scottish centre-forward of arguably equal ability and who was also a prolific goalscorer who enjoyed a phenomenal record during his time at Roker Park. Alongside Halliday in the Roker attack was local lad Bobby Gurney, another brilliant striker who would eventually become the club's record goalscorer. With those two in the attack, Sunderland were always likely to find the target and midway through the first half, after a spell of sustained Newcastle pressure, it was Halliday who opened the scoring. The goal was engineered by Grimshaw who beat Hudspeth down the right before crossing for Halliday to finish from close range.

The second half continued in the same vein with United perhaps creating the better of the opportunities only to be thwarted by McInroy in the Sunderland goal. Then on 70 minutes, Sunderland doubled their advantage with a thrilling solo effort by Death who took on the United defence single-handedly before driving home a terrific left-foot shot high into the net. After that, there was little hope of the visitors salvaging the game as Sunderland continued to defend brilliantly right through to the final whistle.

DAVIE HALLIDAY

SUNDERLAND 5
McKAY (12, 76) HALLIDAY (15, 75) HARGREAVES (25)

NEWCASTLE UNITED 2
BOYD (20) McKENZIE (47)

DATE: 27 October 1928
VENUE: Roker Park
ATTENDANCE: 50,519
COMPETITION: League Division One
REFEREE: Mr. F. H. Harris

SUNDERLAND: McInroy, Murray, England, Clunas, Parker, Andrews, McLean, McKay, Halliday, McInally, Hargreaves.

NEWCASTLE UTD: Wilson, Maitland, Thomson, McKenzie, Hill, McDonald, Boyd, Chambers, Wilkinson, McCurley, Lang.

BACK: HOGG, CLUNAS, McDOUGALL, ENGLAND, McINROY, ANDREWS, MURRAY, REID, COCHRANE. FRONT: LAWLEY, McKAY, HALLIDAY, McNALLY, McLEAN.

A crowd of over 50,000 saw Sunderland finish as comfortable winners in this entertaining derby that was packed with goalmouth action and incident. In an attempt to nullify Sunderland's threat as an attacking force, Newcastle had clearly decided to play an offside game, but their plans backfired badly for at least two of the home side's goals.

Newcastle actually started the game well and for the first ten minutes they had the Sunderland defence stretched with Boyd missing a great opportunity when he fired hopelessly wide with the goal at his mercy. Had United's forwards had more direction in front of goal, it might have given them the initial advantage, for the home defence was looking extremely nervy under pressure.

Sunderland weathered the storm however and after 12 minutes they took the lead with their first real attack of the game. Hargreaves created the chance with a surging run down the left and when he fired over a low cross, McKay swept home a brilliant first-time shot that gave Wilson no chance. Three minutes later, Sunderland doubled their advantage when United's defence tried to play Halliday offside as he chased a ball through the middle, but the referee ignored their appeals and the home centre-forward carried on to finish in style.

The scoreline was perhaps a little harsh on the Magpies, but on 20 minutes they were back in the game when Wilkinson's speculative shot from outside the box smacked against the upright and rebounded straight to Boyd who promptly netted.

Their joy was short-lived however as Sunderland quickly restored their two-goal advantage and again it was United's offside trap that back-fired badly, this time allowing Hargreaves to break through and score.

Their two-goal interval lead perhaps flattered Sunderland, but after only two minutes of the second half the visitors pulled a goal back. Lang set up the chance with a great run down the left and when he pulled his cross back to the edge of the box, McKenzie raced up to hit a 25-yard shot just inside the post to beat McInroy's despairing dive.

For a while, United looked as though they might manage to grab an equaliser, but as the half wore on they faded badly and with Sunderland demonstrating they were clearly the stronger side, two goals in two minutes wrapped up an emphatic victory. Halliday netted his second of the game from close range before McKay again sprung the United's ill-fated offside trap to race through the middle and score number five.

Halliday could well have completed his hat-trick, but on this occasion the referee upheld United's appeals for offside as the Sunderland forward broke through to beat Wilson with a low shot. The 1928-29 season proved to be the highlight of David Halliday's career on Wearside as he finished the campaign with 43 goals in 42 top-flight league games, a club record that stands to this day.

SUNDERLAND 1
GUNSON (12)
NEWCASTLE UNITED 0

DATE: 19 October 1929
VENUE: Roker Park
ATTENDANCE: 58,000
COMPETITION: League Division One
REFEREE: Mr. Mee

SUNDERLAND: Bell, Murray, England, Clunas, McDougall, Allan, Eden, McKay, Halliday, Wood, Gunson.

NEWCASTLE UTD: McInroy, Maitland, Thompson, McKenzie, Hill, Harris, Urwin, Chalmer, Gallacher, McCurley, Lang.

A record crowd of 58,000 had Roker Park bulging at the seams for this eagerly-awaited derby with the majority of Sunderland fans hoping to get their first glimpse of Newcastle's star centre-forward Hughie Gallacher who had missed the previous four derby clashes on Wearside due to international call-ups and suspension.

The appearance of goalkeeper Albert McInroy in United colours was another major talking point, the England international having made a surprise move to join the Magpies two weeks previously for a fee of £2,750.

Whilst those two may have made the pre-match headlines, it was the lesser known Sunderland winger Gordon Gunson who stole the show when he netted the only goal of the game early in the first half. There was only twelve minutes on the clock when he received the ball from Allan, and then took it beyond Maitland on his head before trapping it cleverly.

He then cut in for goal and although the angle looked impossible, he beat McInroy all ends up with a thunderous cross-shot into the corner of the net.

It was a truly brilliant effort by the Sunderland winger and one that sent the massed ranks of Roker fans wild with delight.

McInroy was soon called into action again, making excellent saves, first from McKay and then Halliday as Sunderland began to take control of the game. Early in the second half, Gunson had the ball in the net again, this time with a spectacular diving header, but the goal was ruled out for offside. Then Gallacher suffered a similar fate at the opposite end when the referee disallowed his effort, much to the annoyance of the United players who contested the decision bitterly.

As the game drew to a close, Newcastle threw caution to the wind as they went in search of an equaliser and while Gallacher did have a couple of half-chances, he was well-policed by McDougall who had done a brilliant man-marking job on the United centre-forward. Towards the end, tempers became somewhat frayed and had it not been for the extremely tolerant approach of referee Mee, players from both sides could well have found themselves taking an early bath.

SUNDERLAND 5
EDEN (11, 88) CONNOR (29, 79) GURNEY (71)
NEWCASTLE UNITED 0

DATE: 22 November 1930
VENUE: Roker Park
ATTENDANCE: 26,305
COMPETITION: League Division One
REFEREE: Mr. E. Wood

SUNDERLAND: Middleton, Murray, Shaw, Morris, McDougall, Hastings, Eden, Urwin, Gurney, Leonard, Connor.

NEWCASTLE UTD: McInroy, Richardson, Fairhurst, Naylor, Hill, Weaver, Hutchinson, Chalmers, Lindsay, Devine, Wilkinson.

Sunderland were comfortable winners in this one-sided encounter and while the atrocious weather kept the attendance down to less than half Roker Park's capacity, both sides put on a brave show in extremely testing conditions. United started the game playing against a strong wind and driving rain and faired pretty well in the opening exchanges, but as soon as Eden opened the scoring, the game swung heavily in the home side's favour.

The goal followed some brilliant play from Hastings, Gurney and Connor who combined to set up a chance for Eden which he gleefully headed home. Connor was proving to be Sunderland's star man in attack giving United full-back Richardson a torrid time down the left flank and on 29 minutes, he doubled the home side's advantage.

Gurney created the opening when he deceived the United defence by dummying Eden's cross, allowing it to go to the unmarked Connor whose left foot shot crashed into the corner of the net.

After the break, there was still little evidence of Newcastle as an attacking force and it seemed only a matter of time before Sunderland would increase their advantage. McInroy denied them with a couple of excellent saves, but on 71 minutes, he was helpless to stop Gurney netting Sunderland's third goal of the afternoon.

Eden created the opening when he beat Fairhurst before picking out Urwin who unselfishly set up Gurney to score with the simplest of chances. United's defence was now all at sea and eight minutes later, Connor netted his second goal of the game, firing home in style after Eden's cross had been deflected into his path.

Eden was having a brilliant game on the right wing and two minutes from time he completed the Magpies' misery when he netted number five, driving a terrific shot past McInroy after Connor and Gurney had combined to set up the chance.

At full-time, Sunderland fans headed home wet, but happy, following what had been a truly resounding victory, whereas for United fans, it was very much an afternoon to forget.

JIMMY CONNOR

31

NEWCASTLE UNITED 1
LANG (56)

SUNDERLAND 2
YORSTON (41) GALLACHER (89)

DATE: 9 April 1932
VENUE: St. James' Park
ATTENDANCE: 45,000
COMPETITION: League Division One
REFEREE: Mr. Bob Blake

NEWCASTLE UTD: McInroy, Nelson, Fairhurst, McKenzie, Davidson, Naylor, Boyd, Richardson, Allan, McMenemy, Lang.

SUNDERLAND: Middleton, Murray, Shaw, Hastings, McDougall, Edgar, Temple, Gurney, Yorston, Devine, Gallacher.

This was Sunderland's first derby success on enemy soil for over eight years and was secured in the most dramatic fashion imaginable with the winning goal coming in the dying seconds of the game. The game could never be described as a classic with very little quality football on display for the 45,000 crowd, although Sunderland did produce the more positive attacking approach and were undoubtedly worthy winners.

The first half brought little in the way of goal-mouth action until four minutes before the break when a misunderstanding between McInroy and Fairhurst presented Sunderland with the opening goal. While the United defenders hesitated, Yorston seized onto the loose ball and even though McInroy managed recover to save his first effort, he was beaten when the ball was returned to the middle for the Sunderland forward to head home.

Even then, the United 'keeper managed to palm Yorston's header away, but the referee ruled the ball had crossed the line. Within a minute however, Newcastle were handed a great opportunity to draw level when the referee spotted a handling offence in the box and awarded them a penalty. However, when McKenzie stepped up to take the kick, he drove his effort high over the bar. Then just before the break, Sunderland came close to doubling their advantage when Gallacher beat McInroy with a great low drive only to see his effort hit the foot of the post and rebound to safety.

BENNY YORSTON

The home side began the second half in the ascendancy and it came as no surprise when they drew level on 56 minutes. The goal followed a corner on the right and when the ball broke to Lang, he fired a terrific cross drive past Middleton and into the far corner of the net. For a while it looked as though the game might swing in United's favour, but Sunderland were still looking the more likely side with their controlled attacking play causing endless problems for the home defence.

Nevertheless, the game did look to be heading for a draw until the final minute when Yorston sent Gurney clear on the left and after racing into the box, he presented Gallacher with the easiest of opportunities at the far post. There were strong claims that the goal was offside and United's protests continued after the final whistle as the players and officials were leaving the field, all to no avail of course.

NEWCASTLE UNITED 0
SUNDERLAND 1
GURNEY (5)

DATE: 8 April 1933
VENUE: St. James' Park
ATTENDANCE: 36,000
COMPETITION: League Division One
REFEREE: Mr. Bob Blake

NEWCASTLE UTD: McInroy, Nelson, Fairhurst, McKenzie, Betton, Murray, Boyd, Richardson, Allan, McMenemy, Lang.

SUNDERLAND: Thorpe, Murray, Shaw, Thomson, McDougall, Edgar, Davis, Gallacher, Gurney, Devine, Connor.

A piece of individual brilliance by Sunderland centre-forward Bobby Gurney settled this otherwise dour encounter which produced little to excite the 36,000 crowd. As always, the victory was sweet for Sunderland, but would also be remembered on Tyneside for some time as it effectively ended United's hopes of clinching the league title.

The goal came after only five minutes when Fairhurst attempted to keep the ball in play on the right wing only to lose his footing, allowing Sunderland to gain possession. The ball was played down the right to Gurney who seemed to be well-covered by Betton, but the United defender slipped at the vital moment allowing Gurney to break clear. The Sunderland centre-forward cut in along the goal-line and with everyone expecting a cross, he slotted the ball past McInroy from the narrowest of angles at the near post. It was a brilliant piece of opportunism by Gurney who was fast earning a reputation as one on the top goalscorers in the English game. The Silksworth-born striker would go on to net a record 228 goals for Sunderland and win full international honours for England.

The remainder of the game developed into a midfield battle and with both defences very much in control, clear-cut chances were few and far between. McDougall in particular, had an outstanding game at the heart of the Sunderland defence and carried on bravely to the end after receiving a severe head wound midway through the second half.

Sunderland had always looked the more likely to score, but the best chance of the game fell to Richardson in the closing minutes after excellent work by McMenemy, but the United inside-right shot hopelessly wide from six yards.

BOBBY GURNEY

SUNDERLAND 2
DAVIS (5) SHAW (63 PEN)
NEWCASTLE UNITED 0

DATE: 3 March 1934
VENUE: Roker Park
ATTENDANCE: 32,358
COMPETITION: League Division One
REFEREE: Mr. George Hewitt

SUNDERLAND: Middleton, Murray, Shaw, Thomson, Johnston, Hastings, Davis, Carter, Gurney, Gallacher, Connor.

NEWCASTLE UTD: McPhillips, Nelson, Thomson, Bell, Davidson, Weaver, Boyd, Richardson, Williams, Dennison, Lang.

As a football spectacle, this was a hugely disappointing derby match although, in fairness to both sets of players, the strong wind swirling around Roker Park throughout the game made constructive play almost impossible. Sunderland were certainly worthy winners and could well have won by a much greater margin had it not been for McPhillips in the United goal who made a number of brilliant saves to thwart the Roker attack.

Sunderland took the lead after five minutes when Hastings and Connor exchanged passes to open the Newcastle defence and create an opening for Davis which he gleefully accepted, driving the ball low into the corner of the net. The home side continued to dominate the game and Gallacher had the ball in the net again only to see the effort controversially ruled out for offside. The inside forward's luck got no better a few minutes later when he sustained a bad ankle injury and was forced to play the rest of the game hobbling on the left wing. Soon afterwards, United had a great opportunity to get back into the game when they were awarded a penalty after Richardson had been fouled in the box, but Weaver's shot smacked against the angle of post and bar and rebounded to safety.

After the break, McPhillips continued to deny the Roker attack with a series of excellent saves while at the other end, Middleton performed heroics to deny Williams after Richardson had set up a great scoring opportunity. Midway through the half came the game's second penalty and on this occasion, huge controversy surrounded the incident.

The kick was awarded to Sunderland after a dubious handball by Nelson and was hotly disputed by the United defenders. Justice seemed to have been served when Shaw's kick was saved by McPhillips only for the referee to order the kick to be retaken following encroachment by the United players. This time Shaw made no mistake despite a brave attempt to save by the United 'keeper who

SUNDERLAND'S 1933-34 TEAM PICTURED BELOW THE ROKER END TERRACING.
BACK: HALL, McDOUGALL, HASTINGS, AINSLEY, SHAW, MIDDLETON, MURRAY & EDGAR.
FRONT: JOHNSTON, CONNOR, McNAB, COCHRANE (MANAGER), GURNEY, THOMSON & GALLACHER.

managed to get his hands to the ball, but couldn't prevent it crossing the line. That effectively sealed the game in Sunderland's favour and while United could point to their penalty misfortune, there was no doubt that on the day, the best team won.

The defeat put Newcastle deep in relegation trouble and at the end of the season they lost their top-flight status finishing second bottom in Division One. For Sunderland however, this was the start of a truly golden era for the club that saw them crowned as Football League champions in 1936 and lift the FA Cup for the first time ever a year later.

SUNDERLAND 2
KIRTLEY (17) FORD (34)

NEWCASTLE UNITED 1
MITCHELL (28)

DATE: 26 March 1951
VENUE: Roker Park
ATTENDANCE: 55,150
COMPETITION: League Division One
REFEREE: Mr. B. J. Flanagan

SUNDERLAND: Mapson, Hedley, Hudgell, Watson, Hall, A.Wright, T.Wright, Kirtley, Ford, Shackleton, Reynolds.

NEWCASTLE UTD: Fairbrother, Cowell, Corbett, Stokoe, Brennan, Crowe, Walker, Taylor, Milburn, Hannah, Mitchell.

This game saw Sunderland produce a stirring performance to secure their first victory over their arch-rivals since 1934, the season the Magpies were relegated. Newcastle had returned to the top flight in 1948, two years after top-class football resumed in England following World War Two, and this was Sunderland's sixth attempt to record a victory. On this occasion however, they were much the better side and won the game much more convincingly than the 2-1 scoreline suggests.

The first half was very much a one-sided affair with only desperate defending by the United rearguard preventing an avalanche of goals for the home side, who produced some brilliant attacking play. In particular, Sunderland's star-forward Len Shackleton was at his mercurial best and no doubt eager to put one over on his former club. The man known as 'The Clown Prince of Soccer' had moved to Roker Park in February 1948 and made it well known, that he had little love of the Magpies, often stating: 'I'm not biased against Newcastle - I don't care who beats them!'

Predictably perhaps, it was Shackleton who engineered the opening goal after 17 minutes when he beat two United defenders before setting up a chance for Ford, who seemed to slice his effort only for the ball to roll fortuitously into the path of Kirtley who gave Fairbrother no chance with a low drive. Sunderland continued to dominate, but after 28 minutes United drew level after they were awarded a free-kick just outside the box.

Mitchell took the kick and curled the ball over the Sunderland defensive wall and into the top corner of the net. It was a goal the visitors barely deserved, but it was nevertheless an excellent finish by the Scottish winger. The Magpies' joy was short lived however when six minutes later Sunderland regained the lead after brilliant work by Tommy Wright who weaved his way through the United defence before playing the ball through to Ford. Brennan was in hot pursuit, but Ford's pace took him clear of the United centre-half to finish in some style with a terrific low drive into the corner of the net.

The scoring ended there and while Newcastle did come into the game more in the second period, their only effort of note was when Milburn rounded Mapson only to shoot into the side netting. Then in the closing stages, Tommy Wright came within inches of adding a third goal for the home side when his right-foot shot hit the foot of the post before rebounding to safety.

Overall, Sunderland were worthy winners in a thoroughly entertaining contest and their dominance made a mockery of the sides' relative league positions. For Newcastle, the defeat was a major blow to their hopes of a league and cup double, whereas by contrast, the victory helped Sunderland pull clear of their precarious position near the foot of the table, much to the relief of their supporters.

BACK: ARTHUR WRIGHT, JACK HEDLEY, DICKIE DAVIS, LEN SHACKLETON, BILLY WALSH, IVOR BROADIS, JOHNNY MAPSON, JACK STELLING. FRONT: TOMMY WRIGHT, WILLIE WATSON, TOMMY REYNOLDS.

SUNDERLAND 4
PURDON (33) BINGHAM (38, 52) CHISHOLM (63)

NEWCASTLE UNITED 2
MILBURN (47) MITCHELL (67 PEN)

DATE: 9 October 1954
VENUE: Roker Park
ATTENDANCE: 66,654
COMPETITION: League Division One
REFEREE: Mr. A. Ellis

SUNDERLAND: Fraser, Hedley, McDonald, Anderson, Daniel, Aitken, Bingham, Shackleton, Purdon, Chisholm, Elliott.

NEWCASTLE UTD: S.Mitchell, Cowell, McMichael, Scoular, Stokoe, Crowe, White, Broadis, Milburn, Hannah, R.Mitchell.

BILLY BINGHAM

A crowd of 66,654, Roker Park's third-highest ever attendance, saw Sunderland record a well-deserved victory and move to the top of Division One. The packed terraces saw many youngsters being passed over the heads of supporters to the sanctuary of the perimeter cinder track and mid-way through the first half spectators from the Roker End were allowed to sit alongside the pitch in front of the main stand to ease the crushing on the packed terraces.

Sunderland began the game attacking the Roker End, but it was the visitors who created the first real opening when Hannah attacked down the left, leaving the home defenders in his wake before firing the ball past Fraser. Fortunately for Sunderland, McDonald had raced back and was able to block the ball just short of the line and clear the danger.

Sunderland soon recovered from that early shock however and gradually began to take control of the game with Mitchell in the United goal having to perform heroics on more than one occasion to keep the scoreline blank. However, the deadlock was finally broken on 33 minutes when Bingham crossed to the far post and when Cowell hesitated, Purdon nipped in to squeeze the ball past Mitchell through the narrowest of gaps. Five minutes later, the home side doubled their advantage and this time it was Bingham with a speculative shot from 20 yards that looped over the United 'keeper and into the net.

In the first half there had been little evidence of United as an attacking force, yet two minutes after the restart they were very much back in the game with a stunning goal by Milburn. Broadis began the move and when the ball was played through to the United centre-forward, he stormed into the box to unleash a blistering right-foot drive that gave Fraser no chance. A few minutes later, Shackleton missed a great chance to restore Sunderland's two-goal advantage when he was through on goal after a mesmerising run, but opted to dribble the ball around Mitchell and the United 'keeper was able to make a last-ditch save just short of the line.

The home supporters didn't have to wait long for that third goal however and again it was Bingham who bagged his second of the game when he headed home Elliott's cross after a brilliant run down the left by the Sunderland winger. Then Shackleton almost added his name to the score-sheet with a stunning swerving shot from 30 yards that Mitchell only managed to stop at the second attempt.

Sunderland were now in total control and it came as no surprise when Chisholm netted a fourth after brilliant work by Shackleton. United did pull a goal back when Mitchell netted from the spot after a dubious handball by Aitken, but on the day, they were soundly beaten by a buoyant Sunderland side.

NEWCASTLE UNITED 1
MILBURN (46)

SUNDERLAND 2
FLEMING (43, 89)

DATE: 26 February 1955
VENUE: St. James' Park
ATTENDANCE: 62,835
COMPETITION: League Division One
REFEREE: Mr. A. Ellis

NEWCASTLE UTD: Simpson, Cowell, Batty, Scoular, Stokoe, Casey, Milburn, Broadis, Keeble, Hannah, Mitchell.

SUNDERLAND: Fraser, Hedley, McDonald, Anderson, Daniel, Aitken, Kemp, Fleming, Purdon, Chisholm, Elliott.

CHARLIE FLEMING

A dramatic last-minute goal from Charlie Fleming secured an important victory for Sunderland and kept their title hopes alive, although for long periods in this game, the Wearsiders were very much second best.

Had United taken the opportunities that came their way the scoreline may have made very different reading, the main culprit being centre-forward Vic Keeble who missed three presentable chances. Nevertheless, Sunderland's defence should take great credit for the manner in which they contained the home side's attacks particularly left-half George Aitken who was a rock in the heart of the Roker rearguard.

Having won the toss for United, Scoular decided to take advantage of the strong breeze and it was the United skipper who had the first real attempt on goal, a 20-yard drive that just cleared the crossbar. Soon afterwards Keeble headed weakly from a great position allowing Fraser to palm clear, then on 20 minutes the United centre-forward headed over the bar when it looked easier to score.

As an attacking force, little was seen of Sunderland for most of the opening half perhaps due largely to the absence of Len Shackleton, who somewhat surprisingly had been omitted from the starting line-up. However, it was from a rare attack just before the break that they took the lead when a cross from Elliott was headed back across the face of goal by Kemp allowing Fleming to chest the ball down and turn and shoot past Simpson. The half-time scoreline certainly flattered Sunderland, but within 45 seconds of the restart United were level.

From the kick-off Keeble went on a run through the middle only to be brought down 20 yards from goal. Scoular took the kick and squared it to Milburn who rifled home a low drive that gave Fraser no chance.

From the restart, the game switched quickly to the other end of the park and a stinging shot from Elliott brought out a brilliant save from Simpson. Then Keeble looked to have put the home side in front only to see his header strike Fraser's knee and rebound to safety.

Suddenly the game had developed into an end-to-end affair with Sunderland's attack at last beginning to cause problems for the home defence. However, as the game moved into the closing stages, both sides seemed to have settled for a share of the spoils until Sunderland snatched the points with only seconds remaining. The chance came after Casey had fouled Purdon and when Hedley drove the free-kick into the box, Fleming sent a glancing header into the net, to send the Sunderland supporters home happy.

The victory kept Sunderland in second place, one point behind leaders Wolverhampton Wanderers, but they were unable to sustain their challenge for a seventh league title, finishing the campaign in fourth place, four points behind champions Chelsea.

NEWCASTLE UNITED 0
SUNDERLAND 2
HOLDEN (41, 83)

DATE: 3 March 1956
VENUE: St. James' Park
ATTENDANCE: 61,474
COMPETITION: FA Cup Sixth Round
REFEREE: Mr. R. H. Mann

NEWCASTLE UTD: Simpson, Batty, McMichael, Stokoe, Paterson, Scoular, Milburn, Davies, Keeble, Curry, Mitchell.

SUNDERLAND: Fraser, Hedley, McDonald, Anderson, Daniel, Aitken, Bingham, Fleming, Holden, Elliott, Shackleton.

WILLIE FRASER PUNCHES CLEAR FROM UNITED FORWARDS VIC KEEBLE AND JACKIE MILBURN

There was enormous interest in the weeks leading up to this FA Cup quarter-final tie with unprecedented crowd scenes at St. James' Park when tickets went on sale the week before the game. Having already lifted the trophy three times during the 1950s, United were also reigning FA Cup holders and were widely regarded as red hot favourites to retain English football's most famous trophy, but on the day, it was two goals from centre-forward Bill Holden that saw Sunderland progress to the semi-final and leave Tyneside in a state of shock.

Before the game, a loudspeaker announcement urged United fans to sing 'The Blaydon Races' throughout the game, a request that was not particularly well received by the Sunderland contingent to say the least! Both sides played in changed strips, Newcastle in white shirts and black shorts and Sunderland in an 'Arsenal' style red shirt with white sleeves and black shorts.

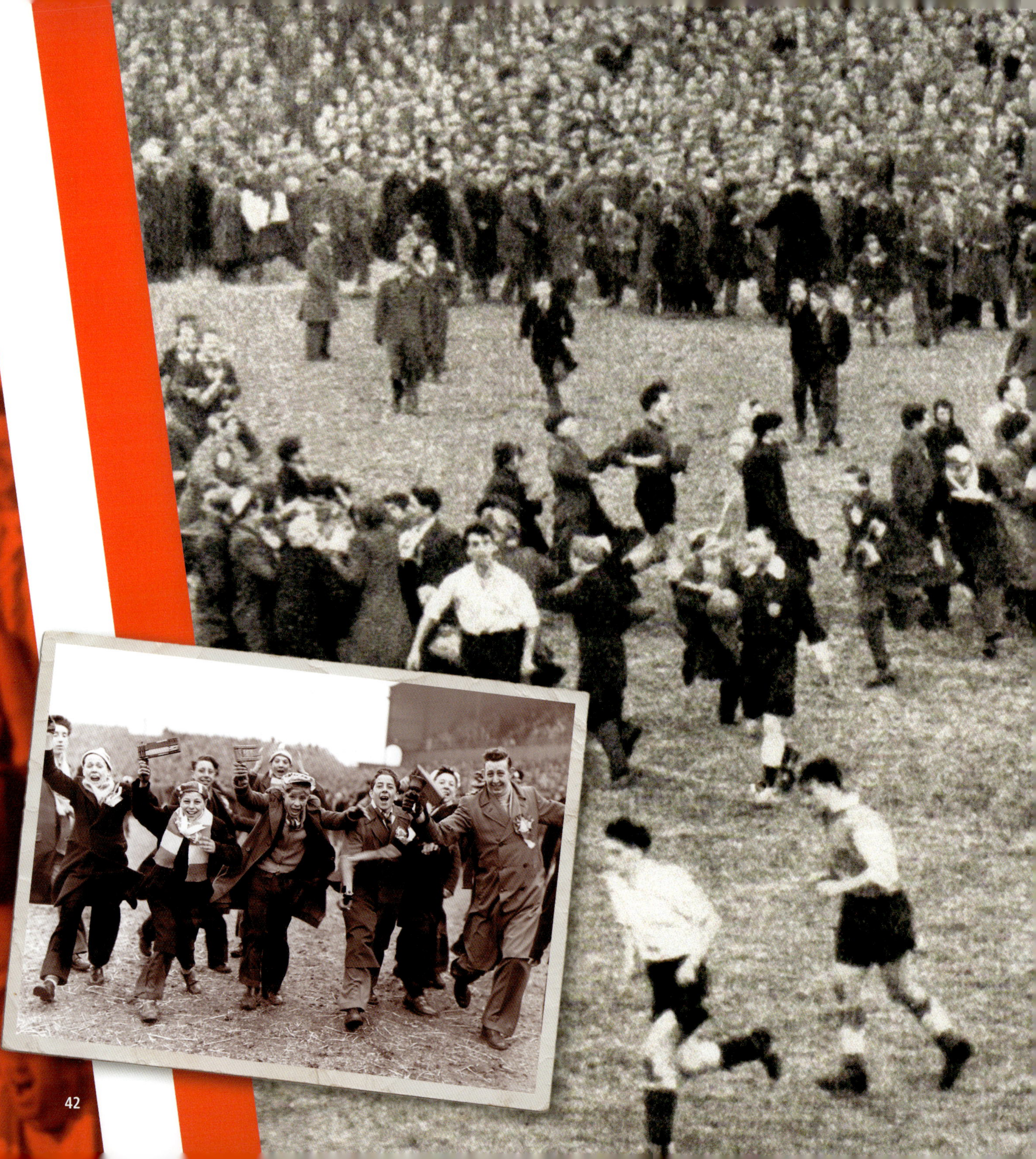

The capacity crowd at St James' Park had paid record receipts of £9,600, but sadly the game failed to live up to its pre-match billing and turned out to be a dour encounter with precious little in the way of quality football on display.

In fairness, the strong, troublesome wind could hardly be described as ideal conditions for football with both sets of players struggling to control the ball and the game was 35 minutes old before the first meaningful shot found the target. This was a terrific drive from Elliott which was brilliantly tipped over the bar by Simpson.

Both sides were beginning to create opportunities with Fleming coming the closest when he raced on to a great through ball by Shackleton, but his shot past Simpson travelled just past the post.

Then four minutes before the break, Sunderland took the lead and again it was Shackleton who set up the chance when he crossed from the left. Simpson seemed to have the ball covered, but was beaten in the air by Holden who sent a looping header over the United 'keeper and into the net.

Soon after the break, United almost grabbed an equaliser when Fraser dropped the ball under challenge from Keeble, but the Sunderland 'keeper quickly recovered to put the ball into touch. At the other end, Holden had a chance after brilliant approach play by Fleming and Bingham, but the Sunderland centre-forward drove his shot well over the top.

Then on 62 minutes, Newcastle missed a golden opportunity to level the tie. Milburn created the opening when he centred from the left for Keeble to head the ball down to Davies in acres of space in front of goal, but the United number eight inexplicably drove the ball hopelessly wide with the goal at his mercy.

Thereafter the Sunderland goal was rarely threatened and seven minutes from time Holden sealed the tie with his second goal of the game. Fleming created the opening with a long ball down the wing which Paterson seemed to have covered only to be out-muscled by Holden who cut in on goal and rounded Simpson before slotting the ball into the empty net.

At the final whistle the celebrating Sunderland fans swarmed onto the pitch to congratulate their heroes. Almost 16,000 had made the journey to Tyneside and celebrations lasted long into the night with a trip to Wembley now almost within touching distance. Sadly, the semi-final turned out to be a major anti-climax for Sunderland who really didn't perform to their full potential on the day and were soundly beaten 3-0 by Birmingham City.

DON REVIE

COLIN GRAINGER

SUNDERLAND 2
REVIE (43) GRAINGER (52)

NEWCASTLE UNITED 0

STAN ANDERSON HEADS FOR GOAL

DATE: 21 September 1957
VENUE: Roker Park
ATTENDANCE: 45,218
COMPETITION: League Division One
REFEREE: Mr. A. W. Luty

SUNDERLAND: Fraser, Hedley, McDonald, Anderson, Aitken, Elliott, Bingham, Revie, Fleming, O'Neill, Grainger.

NEWCASTLE UTD: S.Mitchell, Keith, McMichael, Scoular, Stokoe, Casey, Hill, Davies, Keeble, Curry, R.Mitchell.

Having narrowly escaped relegation the previous season, Sunderland began the 1957-58 campaign with a new manager at the helm in the shape of Alan Brown, a tough disciplinarian who had been appointed in an attempt to reverse the club's ailing fortunes.

The early signs were promising and this Tyne-Wear derby certainly gave Sunderland supporters hope as their team produced an outstanding performance to record a well-deserved victory over their arch-rivals, with skipper Don Revie producing a 'man of the match' display in midfield. Torrential downpours in the hours leading up to the game kept the attendance down to just over 45,000 and the rain was still falling when Revie won the toss and chose to attack the Roker End.

With only six minutes on the clock, Sunderland missed a great opportunity to take the lead when Revie sent O'Neill clear through the middle. Mitchell in the United goal won the race for possession only to drop the ball and leave O'Neill with an open goal, yet the Sunderland inside-left somehow contrived to poke the ball wide from only three yards out. It was a truly amazing miss and one that was greeted with howls of disbelief by the crowd and colleagues alike.

Sunderland fans were cursing their luck again soon afterwards when Fleming came within a whisker of giving the home side the lead with an audacious lob that caught Mitchell off his line, but the ball struck the face of the bar before being gathered by the relieved United 'keeper. Little had been seen of Newcastle as an attacking force, but in a rare breakaway Keeble had the ball in the Sunderland net only to see his effort ruled out for offside.

However, Sunderland were very much in control of the game and deservedly took the lead two minutes before the break. Elliott began the move that saw Fleming racing into the box and when he collided with Mitchell the ball broke clear for Revie to fire into the empty net.

The home fans had to endure an early scare soon after the start of the second half when only stout defending by Fraser, Hedley and McDonald prevented Davies grabbing a equaliser for the Magpies, but on 52 minutes, they were cheering loudly when Grainger doubled Sunderland's advantage.

Bingham created the chance beating Stokoe out on the right before crossing for the left-winger to head home from close range. Even though there was still 38 minutes remaining, that goal pretty much settled the game as a contest and Sunderland could easily have increased their advantage with O'Neill, Revie and Grainger all coming close.

Sadly, this victory was one of the few bright spots in what was otherwise a dismal season for Sunderland Football Club that saw them finish second bottom in Division One and suffer the ignominy of relegation for the first time in the club's long and illustrious history. It would be another six years before top-flight football returned to Roker Park.

SUNDERLAND 3
HERD (19, 82) McPHEAT (76)
NEWCASTLE UNITED 0

DATE: 21 April 1962
VENUE: Roker Park
ATTENDANCE: 57,666
COMPETITION: League Division Two
REFEREE: Mr. A. W. Luty

SUNDERLAND: Montgomery, Irwin, Ashurst, Anderson, Hurley, McNab, Hooper, Herd, Clough, McPheat, Overfield.

NEWCASTLE UTD: Hollins, Keith, McMichael, Wright, Thompson, Dalton, Day, Kerray, Thomas, Allchurch, Fell.

After four years of rebuilding, the 1961-62 season saw Alan Brown's young team finally emerge as serious contenders for a return to the top flight and with four games to go, they were hot on the tail of second-placed Leyton Orient in the Division Two promotion race. The first of these games provided a tough challenge against their arch-rivals from Tyneside, a contest Sunderland simply had to win to keep their hopes alive.

Torrential rain on Wearside meant the game was played in extremely difficult conditions, but that didn't stop both sides producing some thrilling football and whilst the 3-0 scoreline suggests a comfortable victory for Sunderland, the Magpies can take great credit for their performance, particularly early on in the game.

For the first 15 minutes or so, the visitors were arguably the better side, but it was the home team who grabbed the crucial first goal after 19 minutes through Scottish international inside-forward George Herd. The opening was created by Clough who won possession on the edge of the box allowing Herd to pick up the loose ball and race into the box and slot the ball past Hollins in the United goal. Thereafter, Sunderland were pretty much in control and while Montgomery had to be alert to deal with two great efforts from Allchurch, early in the second half, the visitors rarely looked like finding a way back into the game.

Little was seen of United's star striker Barrie Thomas who was completely shut out of the game by Charlie Hurley, who was in outstanding form in the heart of the Sunderland defence.

With 14 minutes remaining Sunderland finally made the game safe when Anderson released Hooper with a brilliant pass and when the right-winger's shot was partially blocked by Hollins, McPheat followed up to push the ball into the empty net. Soon afterwards, Herd netted a third when he received the ball 30 yards out with his back to goal, turned his man and raced to the edge of the box before unleashing a terrific shot which crashed into the net with Hollins helpless.

GEORGE HERD

The result saw Sunderland climb into third place, two points behind Leyton Orient with a game in hand. Home and away victories over Rotherham United in the next two matches meant Sunderland went into their final game of the season at Swansea knowing a victory would clinch promotion. To their credit, they performed valiantly on the day and while a first-half Brian Clough goal gave them hope, a late Swansea equaliser saw them fall at the final hurdle.

JIM MONTGOMERY SAVES FROM UNITED FORWARD BARRY THOMAS

SUNDERLAND 2
ASHURST (43) HERD (81)

NEWCASTLE UNITED 1
TAYLOR (14)

DATE: 9 October 1963
VENUE: Roker Park
ATTENDANCE: 56,903
COMPETITION: League Division Two
REFEREE: Mr. A. Holland

SUNDERLAND: Montgomery, Irwin, Ashurst, Harvey, Hurley, McNab, Usher, Herd, Sharkey, Crossan, Mulhall.

NEWCASTLE UTD: Hollins, Keith, Dalton, Burton, McGrath, Iley, Suddick, Hilley, Thomas, McGarry, Taylor.

Having seen their team miss out on promotion by the narrowest of margins on the final day of the two previous seasons, Sunderland fans were praying for 'third time lucky' as the 1963-64 campaign got under way. The Magpies were also hopeful of a return to the top flight, so the stakes couldn't have been higher as the teams lined up at Roker Park in front of a crowd of almost 57,000, the ground's largest attendance for a mid-week game under floodlights.

The Sunderland team were still without team captain Stan Anderson who had lost his number-four shirt to up-and-coming youngster Martin Harvey. Anderson was the last of the great 'Bank of England' team inherited by manager Alan Brown and he would soon be forced to sever his ties with the club he had joined as a youngster, when Sunderland accepted a bid of £19,000 from Newcastle United, of all teams, for his services. Born in Horden, Anderson came from a family of Sunderland fanatics, so the move was difficult to take to say the least, but in true professional fashion he went on to give great service at St. James' Park and later served Middlesbrough with distinction, becoming one of only a handful of players to have played for North East football's 'big three'.

Taking over as Sunderland skipper was Charlie Hurley, the man manager Alan Brown had built his new-look team around and a player who was already becoming a legend among the Roker Park faithful.

STAN ANDERSON

Hurley was a man who led by example and on this particular night, the Republic of Ireland international was in the thick of the action right from the start having to deal with the physical threat of United striker Ron McGarry. The visitors certainly enjoyed the lion's share of possession in the opening stages and stunned the home crowd with an opening goal after 14 minutes when Taylor latched onto a cross from Suddick before racing into the box to drive the ball past Montgomery.

In typical derby fashion, the game was a feisty affair with no quarter asked or given and as half-time approached, Hurley was forced to leave the field after sustaining a severe head wound in a clash with McGarry. Ironically, it was while their skipper was in the treatment room that Sunderland equalised, although the goal could hardly have come from a more unlikely source. They won a free-kick on the left, 30 yards from goal and when Ashurst stepped up to take the kick, he fired in a terrific drive which eluded everyone in the penalty area before crashing into the back of the Fulwell End net with Hollins helpless.

Ashurst went onto play 458 games for Sunderland, a record for an outfield player that still stands to this day, yet in all that time, he only managed four goals! Not surprisingly, it was this particular goal that would never be forgotten by Len, although in his autobiography 'Left Back in Time' he was honest enough to confess that his stunning low drive had actually been an intended cross!

"When I was in the treatment room getting patched up, I heard the huge roar so I knew we'd equalised. When I asked who scored, someone said: 'Len Ashurst.' I said to Johnny Watters, our physio, 'Bloody hell Johnny, there's something wrong with my hearing, I think I must be suffering from concussion, Len Ashurst never scores!'."

CHARLIE HURLEY

There was a huge cheer from the Sunderland fans when a patched-up Hurley led his team out for the second half, as the home side set about the business of winning two vital promotion points. Throughout the second period they dominated the play, but United were defending in depth and there were only nine minutes remaining when Herd finally breached their rear-guard to win the match with a brilliant piece of skill. Mulhall started the move on the left and when he played the ball in, Herd won possession just inside the box before turning to unleash a terrific half-volley that fairly screamed into the net.

The victory was no more than Sunderland deserved. It reinforced their position alongside the Division Two promotion front-runners, a place they held throughout a truly memorable season, before finally finishing in second place behind Leeds United, securing a long-awaited return to the top flight.

49

SUNDERLAND 2
HERD (49) O'HARE (66)
NEWCASTLE UNITED 0

DATE: 3 January 1966
VENUE: Roker Park
ATTENDANCE: 54,668
COMPETITION: League Division One
REFEREE: Mr. J. Carr

SUNDERLAND: Montgomery, Parke, Ashurst, Harvey, Hurley, Baxter, Herd, Elliott, O'Hare, Moore, Mulhall. **SUB:** Hellawell.

NEWCASTLE UTD: Marshall, Craig, Burton, Moncur, McGrath, Iley, Napier, Bennett, Thompson, Hilley, Robson. **SUB:** Penman.

JIM BAXTER

This game was rearranged from the previous week when the Roker Park pitch had been declared unfit for play due to frozen conditions. However, the fixture still managed to attract a crowd of over 54,000 including a large contingent from Tyneside, although it would seem that one or two high-spirited United fans had actually been in the ground the night before.

Apparently on the morning of the game, the Roker Park groundsmen were about to start their pre-match preparations when they discovered that both sets of goalposts had been painted with black and white stripes. Fortunately, after a few hastily applied coats of white paint, everything was back to normal by the time kick-off arrived!

Making his first-ever appearance in a Tyne-Wear derby was Jim Baxter, Sunderland's recent signing from Rangers and regarded by many as one of the finest midfield players in the game. While 'Slim Jim' lacked consistency, on his day he could destroy teams, particularly with his vast array of passing skills from a left foot often referred to as a magic wand! Unfortunately for Newcastle, on this particular day, Baxter put in an outstanding performance which was later described by one national newspaper as 'poetry in motion'.

Sunderland began the game attacking the Fulwell End and came close to taking the lead when Parke went on a great run down the right before crossing for Moore to send in a terrific header that thumped against the bar.

Soon afterwards however, Sunderland's hopes received a severe blow when Hurley was forced to leave the field with a head injury after an aerial collision with Moncur. Mike Hellawell came off the bench to replace him and in doing so became the first-ever Sunderland substitute to be used in a Tyne-Wear derby.

After a goalless first half, Sunderland deservedly took the lead four minutes into the second period when Baxter split the United defence with a great ball which Moore flicked on to send Herd clear just inside the United half. There was still a lot for Herd to do, but he kept his composure and raced in the box to beat Marshall with a terrific rising shot. Surprisingly, this brought little response from United who had been almost anonymous as an attacking force and it came as no surprise when O'Hare doubled the home side's advantage on 66 minutes. In fairness, there was an element of luck surrounding the goal when Marshall appeared to have O'Hare's shot covered only for a wicked deflection off Moncur to leave him stranded. That effectively finished the game as a contest and Sunderland could easily have added to their score as they cruised to a comfortable victory. The points were a welcome relief for their fans in an otherwise disappointing season that saw their team constantly flirting with relegation, eventually finishing in 19th place, just three points above the drop zone.

NEWCASTLE UNITED 0
SUNDERLAND 3
MULHALL (7) MARTIN (42) O'HARE (79)

DATE: 29 October 1966
VENUE: St. James' Park
ATTENDANCE: 58,740
COMPETITION: League Division One
REFEREE: Mr. K. Stokes of Nottinghamshire

NEWCASTLE UTD: Hollins, Craggs, Clark, Moncur, Thompson, Iley, Robson, McGarry, Davies, Hilley, Suddick. **SUB:** Kettleborough.

SUNDERLAND: Montgomery, Irwin, Ashurst, Todd, Kinnell, Harvey, Herd, O'Hare, Martin, Baxter, Mulhall. **SUB:** Elliott.

This victory over their arch-rivals saw Sunderland produce their best performance of the season and finally end a disastrous run of 23 away games without a win. All the pre-match headlines surrounded Newcastle's new signing Wyn Davies, an £80,000 buy from Bolton Wanderers, who was making his debut for the Magpies, but the Welsh international was so well policed by Sunderland's George Kinnell that he posed little threat to the Sunderland goal. Kinnell was one of six Scots in the Sunderland team, in fact their entire forward line had all been born north of the border!

It took Sunderland just seven minutes to make the breakthrough with a superb solo-effort from left-winger George Mulhall who cut in from the left to leave Hollins helpless with a superb shot that curled just inside the far post. Sunderland continued to dominate throughout the opening half and the home crowd were stunned into silence three minutes before half-time when they doubled their lead. Ashurst gained possession out on the left just inside the United half and when he floated a long cross into the box, Martin rose to power home a thumping header.

Throughout the second half, the home fans were becoming increasingly restless as their team struggled to break down the Sunderland rearguard where Kinnell in particular was in outstanding form. United's sole tactic seemed to be to hit long hopeful balls looking for the head of their new striker, but unlike many legendary Newcastle centre-forwards of the past, Davies had a debut very much to forget. With Baxter orchestrating proceedings in the middle of the park, the visitors were always in total control and it was from one of the Scottish international's defence splitting passes that the visitors created the opening for the third goal. Baxter's cross-field pass was inch perfect for Mulhall who left Craggs in his wake as he raced down the left wing before crossing low into the box where O'Hare beat Moncur to drive the ball low into the net from 12 yards.

Given Sunderland's recent away form this was a truly remarkable victory and to achieve it with so much in reserve made it an afternoon to savour for the large contingent of fans who had travelled from Wearside.

SUNDERLAND 3
KERR (56, 72) MULHALL (88)
NEWCASTLE UNITED 0

DATE: 4 March 1967
VENUE: Roker Park
ATTENDANCE: 50,442
COMPETITION: League Division One
REFEREE: Mr. L. Hamer

SUNDERLAND: Montgomery, Irwin, Harvey, Todd, Kinnell, Baxter, Kerr, O'Hare, Martin, Herd, Mulhall. **SUB:** Gauden.

NEWCASTLE UTD: Marshall, Craig, Clark, Elliott, McNamee, Moncur, Robson, McGarry, Davies, Hilley, Robson. **SUB:** Noble.

This victory gave Sunderland a rare seasonal double over their arch-rivals and maintained a run of excellent form that had seen them pull clear of the Division One relegation zone. The upturn in their fortunes had coincided with the arrival on the first-team scene of 19-year-old Bobby Kerr who made a sensational debut when he netted a last-minute winner against Manchester City at Roker Park.

Spotted by Charlie Ferguson, Kerr was just one of a production line of talented youngsters from north of the border spotted by the Sunderland chief scout, many of whom would go on to give the club great service in the years ahead.

As in the game at St. James Park earlier in the season, Sunderland fielded an all-Scottish forward line and again they recorded an emphatic 3-0 victory. Unbeaten in their previous nine league and cup games, Sunderland totally dominated the game from the off, yet amazingly, the scoreline remained blank at the interval. This was largely due to some resolute defending by the United rearguard although Sunderland should really have been in front as a number of presentable chances went begging.

Since his debut, Kerr had netted a remarkable five goals in nine games and perhaps not surprisingly, given this amazing run of form, it was the young Scot who opened the scoring eleven minutes into the second half. The goal came from a mistake by McNamee who attempted a back-pass to Marshall only for Kerr to nip in and send a glancing header past the United 'keeper and into the net.

It was a brilliant piece of opportunism by Kerr and 16 minutes later he was at it again, this time latching on to a Mulhall cross-shot to fire the ball home. Amazingly, a few minutes later, the youngster had the ball in the net again, but was denied what would have been a truly memorable hat-trick by a dubious offside decision by the linesman.

With two minutes to go, Mulhall completed the scoring to round off a great team performance, but, not surprisingly, it was young Bobby Kerr who made all the post-match headlines. Sadly however, his fairytale baptism into top-class football soon came to a shuddering halt when he sustained a broken leg following a collision with Norman Hunter in a fifth round FA Cup-tie at Roker Park a week later. After suffering the same injury in a comeback game at Ashington, Kerr made a full recovery and went on to enjoy a great career in the game, the highlight of which was undoubtedly lifting the FA Cup for Sunderland in 1973.

"The one thing I remember about that game was the incredible atmosphere. The noise was unbelievable and for a young kid like me to bag two goals against the arch-enemy really was the stuff of dreams. Mind you, I really should have been walking off with the match ball because I'm certain that third goal was legitimate and the linesman got it badly wrong!"

BOBBY KERR

NEWCASTLE UNITED 1
CONNELLY (50)

SUNDERLAND 4
ROWELL (6, 25, 62) ENTWHISTLE (71)

DATE: 24 February 1979
VENUE: St. James' Park
ATTENDANCE: 34,733
COMPETITION: League Division Two
REFEREE: Pat Partridge

NEWCASTLE UTD: Hardwick, Brownlie, Nattrass, Martin, Bird, Blackley, Shoulder, Walker, With, Hibbitt, Connelly.
SUB: Mitchell.

SUNDERLAND: Siddall, Henderson, Bolton, Arnott, Clarke, Elliott, Chisholm, Rostron, Entwhistle, Lee, Rowell.
SUB: Docherty.

If ever a Sunderland player 'lived the dream', then it was most certainly Gary Rowell, whose almost one-man demolition of the Magpies on this incredible afternoon at St. James' Park guaranteed him legendary status on Wearside forever and a day. As a self-confessed red and white fanatic from his earliest days, Gary had already fulfilled his lifetime ambition by playing for the club he loved, but to score a hat-trick against the Magpies in their own back yard well, that really was 'Roy of the Rovers' stuff!

The seventies had seen both Sunderland and Newcastle United slip into English football's second tier and both were desperate for a quick return to the top flight when they met for this eagerly awaited encounter. Under caretaker-manager Billy Elliott, Sunderland were enjoying something of a revival and were much better placed lying in fifth position, whereas the Magpies had slipped into mid-table following a run of poor results.

Sunderland started the game attacking the Leazes End and needed only six minutes to breach the United rearguard when Clarke's free-kick was headed on by Chisholm and then Rostron for Rowell to turn the ball home from close range in typical predatory fashion.

ROWELL SCORES THE FIRST AFTER ONLY SIX MINUTES

The goal inspired Sunderland to a spell of relentless attacking play that had United defending desperately, but there was little they could do on 25 minutes when Rowell netted his second with a superb finish. Arnott created the opening with a perfectly judged pass that split the home defence to send the Sunderland striker racing through to beat Hardwick with a brilliant low drive from the edge of the box.

At the break, United had looked a beaten side, but five minutes into the second half, Connelly gave them a lifeline when he headed home Walker's left-wing cross. Sunderland quickly gained the initiative however and on 62 minutes they regained their two-goal advantage to effectively make the game safe. Henderson attacked down the right and when he was upended by Mitchell, the referee had no hesitation in pointing to the spot. Rowell stepped up to take the kick and coolly slotted the ball into the corner of the net to send the massed ranks of Sunderland fans at the opposite end of the ground into sheer ecstasy! No sooner had their cheers died down than Lee had the ball in the United net again, only for referee Pat Partridge to bring the play back and award a free-kick to Sunderland! Soon afterwards, the fourth goal did arrive, when Rowell beat Hardwick with a cross from the right for Entwhistle to head home at the far post, even though the ball might well have crossed the line anyway.

It had been a truly memorable day for everyone associated with Sunderland Football Club, but of course, none more so than Gary Rowell who quickly became a cult hero with the club's supporters who would regularly chant 'We all live in a Gary Rowell World' to the tune of the Beatles' 'Yellow Submarine'!

After the match, Argos of the Footy Echo commented:

"Sunderland had the edge all the way through. They had the power in defence and midfield and, of course, where it mattered most, in turning command into goals, they had Gary Rowell. His cool, professional attitude was both lesson and inspiration to everyone. Rowell's pride in his own achievement was certainly shared by his dad, Jack, himself a former Sunderland player, who was still jumping for joy long after the game had finished!"

United manager Bill McGarry was equally complimentary about Sunderland's hat-trick hero:

"Rowell is quite simply a gift. You never see him, he just scores goals."

Sadly, Sunderland's season was to end in major disappointment when they missed out on a return to the top flight by the narrowest of margins. The promotion chase had gone to the final game at Wrexham where a 2-1 victory appeared to have clinched second place, only for rivals Stoke City to grab a dramatic last-minute goal and deny Sunderland their moment of glory.

NUMBER TWO FOR GARY

"*My heart was pounding when I stepped up to take the penalty and I'll always remember how I felt when the ball hit the back of the net and then watching the dejected Newcastle fans streaming out of the ground, while ours were going wild with delight at the other end of the ground. All those hours of practice on the training ground really did pay dividends! My only disappointment that day was that I never managed to get my hands on the match ball. Apparently one of the officials had claimed it, but of all my hat-tricks, that was the ball I really wanted!*"

GARY ROWELL

NEWCASTLE UNITED 2
BOAM (76) SHOULDER (88)

SUNDERLAND 2
BROWN (75, 90+4)

SUNDERLAND WON 7-6 ON PENALTIES

DATE: 5 September 1979
VENUE: St. James' Park
ATTENDANCE: 30,553
COMPETITION: League Cup Second Round Second Leg
REFEREE: Pat Partridge

NEWCASTLE UTD: Hardwick, Brownlie, Davies, Martin, Barton, Boam, Shoulder, Pearson, With, Hibbitt.
SUB: Cartwright.

SUNDERLAND: Siddall, Whitworth, Bolton, Clarke, Elliott, Ashurst, Buckley, Rostron, Brown, Robson, Rowell.
SUB: Chisholm.

With Tyneside still smarting from Gary Rowell's almost one-man demolition of their team six months earlier, Newcastle supporters were given a great opportunity for early revenge when the two sides were paired in the League Cup Second Round early in the following season.

The tie was a two-legged affair with the first encounter taking place at Roker Park and midway through the second half Sunderland appeared to be in the driving seat after Wilf Rostron and Pop Robson had given them a two goal lead, but Newcastle were to level the tie with two late goals and in the dying seconds were unlucky not to get the winner.

Having home advantage, the Magpies were now firm favourites to progress to the next round and in the opening 45 minutes only the brilliance of Barry Siddall in the Sunderland goal kept them at bay. With the game goalless at the break there was no hint of the drama that was about to unfold in the second period.

Again, United started the stronger and Pearson was desperately unlucky not to give them the lead when he sent in a tremendous header that hit the underside of the bar before being scrambled to safety. Soon afterwards, the play switched to the other end and Ashurst almost had Sunderland in front when he unleashed a terrific right-foot shot which struck Boam on its way and had Hardwick turning in mid-air to make a magnificent save.

Then, with about 15 minutes to go, the tie exploded into life when Sunderland were awarded a free-kick just outside the United penalty area. Rostron took the kick and floated the ball to the far post where Brown, from what seemed an impossible angle, beat Hardwick with a superb header. Within minutes however, United were level when Boam, lending his weight to the attack, met a corner at the near post to send a glancing header wide of Siddall and into the net. Amazingly, with only a couple of minutes remaining United snatched what looked to be the winner and again it was a header from a set-piece, this time from Shoulder after Martin had flicked on a Hibbitt corner.

But this was to be Alan Brown's night and with the game deep into stoppage time, he silenced the celebrating black and white hordes with a stunning strike. There seemed to be little danger as he received a long hopeful ball from Clarke, but a brilliant turn took him clear of Boam to send a low right-foot shot wide of Hardwick and just inside the post.

Thirty minutes of extra-time followed and while Sunderland came closest when Robson saw a magnificent header from a Buckley cross come back into play from the inside of the far post, the scores were still level at the final whistle. Both managers tried to rally their troops as they gathered on the half-way line in readiness for the dreaded penalty shoot-out.

BROWN'S STOPPAGE-TIME EQUALISER

Sunderland's regular penalty-taker was Gary Rowell, but he had been substituted during extra-time, so manager Ken Knighton handed his job to Alan Brown. One by one, the penalties flew in and then, with the score at 6-6, Brown stepped up to take his kick, which he duly dispatched with some power off the underside of the bar. With tension now almost at breaking point, United's Jim Pearson stepped up, but placed his shot too close to Barry Siddall who palmed the ball clear before racing down the pitch to be mobbed by his delighted colleagues!

It had been an outstanding performance by Sunderland and in particular for their striker Alan Brown who had scored both goals as well as netting the vital penalty, yet he recalls an amazing confrontation with assistant manager Frank Clark in the dressing room after the game:

"I was feeling quite chuffed and as we were leaving the pitch I picked up the match ball thinking 'I might not have scored a hat-trick, but two goals and a penalty is as near as I'll ever get on this ground, so I'm having this.' Anyway, back in the dressing room, we were all celebrating when Frank Clark, our assistant manager, came storming over and shouted, 'What the hell are you doing with that?', snatching the ball off me, 'don't be so bloody stupid - that wasn't a proper hat-trick!' At the time, I was just speechless. We'd just achieved a magnificent result and all the lads were on cloud nine, yet there was Frank, making a right song and dance about the match ball - bloody ridiculous!"

59

SUNDERLAND 1
CUMMINS (73)
NEWCASTLE UNITED 0

DATE: 5 April 1980
VENUE: Roker Park
ATTENDANCE: 41,752
COMPETITION: League Division Two
REFEREE: Ken Walmsley

SUNDERLAND: Turner, Whitworth, Hinnegan, Clarke, Hindmarch, Elliott, Arnott, Rowell, Brown, Robson, Cummins.
SUB: Dunn.

NEWCASTLE UTD: Hardwick, Carney, Davies, Cassidy, Boam, Barton, Shoulder, Cartwright, Withe, Hibbitt, Shinton.
SUB: Walker.

Having suffered the disappointment of narrowly missing out on promotion the previous season, Sunderland signalled their determination to succeed this time around by breaking the club's transfer record no fewer than three times to add quality reinforcements to manager Ken Knighton's squad.

First to arrive was centre-forward John Hawley, a £200,000 signing from Leeds United and he was followed later in the campaign by Stan Cummins from Middlesbrough for £300,000 together with the club's first-ever South American player, Claudio Marangoni who arrived on Wearside from San Lorenzo for a fee of £320,000.

By the time this Easter Monday fixture came around, both club's were in contention for promotion, although Newcastle's form had dipped following their 3-1 Tyne-Wear derby victory earlier in the season and it was now Sunderland who were considered as promotion favourites. Nevertheless, the match was very much a 'four-pointer' with the Magpies desperate to get their promotion campaign back on track. Sadly, as kick-off time approached, there were numerous violent clashes between rival fans in the streets surrounding Roker Park and these continued on the terraces throughout the game.

While Sunderland were without new signings Hawley and Marangoni who were both sidelined with injuries, they were the better side in what turned out to be a nail-biting encounter played in typical derby fashion with no quarter asked or given. With both defences in control, there were few clear-cut chances being created by either side and as the game headed into its closing stages, a goalless draw looked the most likely outcome. Then with 17 minutes remaining, Sunderland attacked down the right and when Rowell crossed, Hardwick dropped the ball at the near post allowing Cummins to swivel and turn the ball over the line from close range before racing away in celebration.

In the closing minutes United pressed forward looking for an equaliser, but the Roker rearguard held firm to ensure a vital victory to keep their promotion ambitions on track. Again, the outcome of the season would go to the final game, but this time a 2-0 victory over West Ham on a memorable night at Roker Park secured second place in Division Two and a return to the top flight.

STAN CUMMINS SCORES THE WINNER

ERIC GATES NETS
THE OPENING GOAL

NEWCASTLE UNITED 0
SUNDERLAND 2
GATES (13) GABBIADINI (85)

DATE: 16 May 1990
VENUE: St. James' Park
ATTENDANCE: 32,199
COMPETITION: Division Two Play-Off Semi-Final Second Leg
REFEREE: George Courtney

NEWCASTLE UTD: Burridge, Bradshaw, Stimson, Aitken, Anderson, Scott, Brock, Askew, Quinn, McGhee, Kristensen.
SUBS: Dillon, O'Brien.

SUNDERLAND: Norman, Kay, Agboola, Bracewell, Bennett, MacPhail, Owers, Armstrong, Gates, Gabbiadini, Hawke.
SUBS: Heathcote, Hauser.

For atmosphere, passion and no small degree of violence, few derby matches can compare with the Tyne-Wear showdown in the Division One Play-Off semi-final at St. James' Park in 1990. It was a night when Sunderland recorded one of their greatest-ever victories on enemy soil, but it was a bitter blow that many Magpie supporters simply couldn't take as St. James' Park erupted into a cauldron of pure hatred.

Having held Sunderland to a goalless draw at Roker Park in the first leg a few days earlier, Newcastle were red hot favourites to progress through to the Wembley final, with few people outside of Wearside giving Denis Smith's side a chance. The game at Roker had been an uneventful affair with United content to play a containing game in readiness for the second leg. However, in the final minute, the game exploded into life when Marco Gabbiadini was upended in the box and Sunderland were awarded a penalty.

The normally ever-sure Paul Hardyman stepped up to take the kick, but his poorly-hit shot was parried by John Burridge and, as the United keeper dove to gather the rebound, Hardyman carried through prompting ugly scenes as both sets of players piled in.

When order was restored, the Sunderland full-back was shown the red card and when the final whistle sounded moments later, the joyous Newcastle players raced to the Roker End to join their celebrating fans.

However, the missed spot-kick might well have worked to Sunderland's advantage, because the Newcastle players and their supporters clearly thought they had struck a massive psychological blow. Even the press had more or less written Sunderland off after the game at Roker, but there was an air of quiet confidence surrounding Denis Smith's side as they headed up to Tyneside for the second leg the following week.

Despite the optimism in the Sunderland camp, few pundits gave Denis Smith's men a chance, but on the night, his team rose to new heights to produce a performance of epic proportions. The first goal was always going to be crucial and had Mark McGhee's early effort gone in instead of clipping the outside of Tony Norman's right-hand post it might have been a different story.

Instead, it was the visitors who broke the deadlock in the 13th minute with a typical striker's goal from Eric Gates, forcing the ball home from close range after a great right-wing cross from Gary Owers.

On the night, Sunderland were by far the more composed and inventive side and almost doubled their lead when Gabbiadini's pace unlocked the pedestrian home defence to set up Ower's, only for Burridge in the United goal to produce a brilliant one-handed save.

As the game entered it's final stages the home side threw caution to the wind and bombarded the Sunderland penalty area with high balls, but the Sunderland defence held firm.

MARCO GABBIADINI SEALS THE WIN LATE IN THE GAME

Then with only five minutes remaining, Gabbiadini played a delicate one-two with Gates on the edge of the box before racing clear to drive a brilliant left foot shot past Burridge to send the Sunderland fans packed behind the goal into sheer ecstasy!

It was a fantastic strike by the Sunderland forward, but as the Sunderland players joined their fans in celebration, ugly scenes began to develop at the Gallowgate End and before the game had restarted hundreds of United fans had poured onto the field. It was some minutes before police and stewards managed to clear the pitch and allow referee George Courtney to restart proceedings. But moments later, after a second invasion, he was forced halt the game and usher the players to the safety of the dressing room.

As Sunderland full-back John Kay recalled:

"It really was quite frightening, but our biggest worry was that the referee would abandon the game and we'd have to replay the match. Fortunately, George Courtney knew exactly what the Newcastle fans were trying to do and quickly came into our dressing room to reassure us. 'Listen lads,' he said, 'If those so-called supporters think I'm going to abandon this game they've got another thing coming. Even if I've got to stay here until midnight to see it through then I will, make no mistake about that!'"

For almost twenty minutes the sickening scenes out on the pitch continued as Newcastle fans battled with overworked police, who suffered dozens of casualties. Missiles were thrown, hoardings ripped up, and people were carried away on stretchers as the marauding hooligans attempted to reach the Sunderland end of the ground. Fortunately, the thin blue line of policemen stretched across the Leazes End penalty area prevented them reaching their prey and stopped what undoubtedly would have been a bloodbath.

Eventually, order was restored allowing the teams to go through the three or four minutes that remained, before racing to the sanctuary of the dressing rooms for the final time. Not surprisingly, the violence continued long into the night on Tyneside, but by then the Sunderland team and their supporters were back home on Wearside celebrating a truly memorable victory.

A banner displayed at Sunderland's first home game the following season said it all, it read:

Newcastle United 0 Sunderland 2

Some people are on the pitch, they think it's all over - IT IS NOW!

By now, Sunderland were back in the top flight, albeit by the most fortuitous of routes. Having lost the Play-Off final to Swindon Town, they were subsequently promoted when the Wiltshire club was stripped of their promotion after being found guilty of financial irregularities.

65

NEWCASTLE UNITED 1
DYER (28)

SUNDERLAND 2
QUINN (64) PHILLIPS (75)

DATE: 25 August 1999
VENUE: St. James' Park
ATTENDANCE: 36,600
COMPETITION: Premier League
REFEREE: Graham Poll

NEWCASTLE UTD: Wright, Barton, Domi, Solano, Goma, Dabizas, Dyer, Maric, Robinson, McClen, Speed.
SUBS: Ferguson, Green, Harper, Hughes, Shearer.

SUNDERLAND: Sorensen, Makin, Gray, McCann, Bould, Butler, Summerbee, Rae, Quinn, Phillips, Schwarz.
SUBS: Ball, Dichio, Helmer, Marriott, Oster.

Sunderland went into this match as massive underdogs as they attempted to record their first victory over their arch-rivals for nine long years. Promoted from Division One the season before, Peter Reid's team were still finding their feet in the Premier League, but this game would prove to be a launching pad for a great campaign that saw them finish in a commendable seventh place.

Their strikers Niall Quinn and Kevin Phillips had taken the Championship by storm and their goalscoring exploits would continue in the top flight with Phillips finishing the campaign with 30 goals and picking up the Golden Shoe Award as the highest scorer in the top European Leagues.

Most of the immediate pre-match discussion surrounded United manager Ruud Gullit's decision to relegate his star strikers Alan Shearer and Duncan Ferguson to the bench, an unpopular decision with home supporters that would soon haunt the former Dutch international and a one that ultimately brought his tenure in the St. James' Park hot-seat to an end a few days after the game.

NIALL QUINN HEADS THE EQUALISER

67

CHRIS MAKIN

ALEX RAE

Newcastle were also faced with something of a goalkeeping crisis and had been forced plug the gap by signing former Northern Ireland international 'keeper Tommy Wright on a month's loan from Manchester City.

Torrential rain had swept across Tyneside during the hours leading up to kick-off and continued throughout the game as both sides struggled to come to terms with the treacherous conditions. Sunderland began the game attacking the Gallowgate End and were first to threaten when Summerbee broke clear on the right, but his low cross was turned away for a corner by Barton with Phillips waiting to pounce. It was closer still soon afterwards when Phillips whipped in a vicious cross from the left and Quinn was inches away as he slid in at the far post before colliding with Wright who required attention before play could be resumed.

Sunderland had certainly enjoyed the lion's share of possession in the opening stages, but on 28 minutes, United broke out of defence to open the scoring with a well-worked goal. It was Paul Robinson, a former-Sunderland season ticket holder, who created the opening sending Dyer clear to beat Sorensen, chipping the ball over the advancing Sunderland 'keeper. It was a lead that the home side scarcely deserved, but they held on to the interval as Sunderland pushed forward searching for an equaliser.

The conditions were clearly deteriorating as the second half got underway with the ball frequently holding up in the large pools of water that were beginning to develop around the St. James' Park pitch. Robinson appeared to be in with a chance when a long ball down the right sent him clear into the box, but the conditions favoured Sunderland as the ball skidded off the turf and into the hands of Sorensen.

Play then switched quickly to the other end with Phillips racing through the middle only to be crowded out by the United defenders. Then Summerbee picked out Quinn with an excellent cross to the far post, but the Irish international could only direct his header well wide of the target.

There was a huge roar from the home supporters on 57 minutes when Ferguson was brought on to replace Robinson, but five minutes later they were shocked into stunned silence as Sunderland grabbed a deserved equalizer. A feature of the visitor's play had been the crossing ability of Summerbee and it was from a free-kick out on the right that the Sunderland winger picked out Quinn at the near post. The striker appeared to be closely marked, but he somehow managed to hold off the defender to send a backward glancing header low into the net at the far post.

69

SUPERKEV AND ALEX RAE CELEBRATE AT THE FINAL WHISTLE

KEVIN BALL

Five minutes later, Peter Reid made his first substitution bringing on Kevin Ball in place of Stefan Schwarz who had put in a sterling shift in midfield. A few minutes later, the home fans, who had been screaming for the introduction of Alan Shearer since the break, finally got the wish as their star striker entered the fray.

He was soon in the thick of the action, but when he lost possession out on the right, the ball was crossed into the box where Phillips was clear. The chance seemed to have gone when Wright blocked his first effort forcing the ball wide, but the Sunderland striker recovered to turn and send a delightful chip over the United 'keeper and into the net to send the Sunderland fans behind the goal wild with delight.

After that, there was only going to be one winner, although Sunderland supporters had to endure one amazing scare in the dying minutes when a thunderous Kevin Ball challenge 30 yards from goal saw the ball fly towards the Sunderland net with Sorensen stranded. Fortunately, the ball struck to the top of the crossbar and rebounded to safety!

At the final whistle, the 850 or so Sunderland fans who had been fortunate enough to obtain tickets, joined their players in celebration of a truly memorable victory, while back on Wearside, where the game had been beamed back to the Stadium of Light, joyous celebrations continued long into the night.

"The 'keeper saved my first shot, but it came out towards me and I was looking for Niall, but I could barely see him because it looked like he was surrounded by three of four of their players. I just thought I would try to turn it into the top corner thinking that if it didn't come off then it might slice to Niall, but as it turned out I got a clean contact and it went in perfectly!"

KEVIN PHILLIPS

"For me as a manager, it's a great three points, but for our fans, I know it's a little more than that. And I'd like to think that the performance was for them. They've stuck by us through thick and thin for a few seasons now and they deserve this. That game was for them."

PETER REID

NEWCASTLE UNITED 1
SPEED (4)

SUNDERLAND 2
HUTCHISON (67) QUINN (75)

DATE: 18 November 2000
VENUE: St. James' Park
ATTENDANCE: 52,030
COMPETITION: Premier League
REFEREE: Graham Poll

NEWCASTLE UTD: Given, Solano, Domi, Lee, Hughes, Caldwell, Dyer, Acuna, Shearer, Bassedas, Speed.
SUBS: Harper, Griffin, Barton, Cordone, LuaLua.

SUNDERLAND: Sorensen, Makin, Gray, Williams, Craddock, Thome, Hutchison, Rae, Quinn, Phillips, Kilbane.
SUBS: Macho, Varga, Arca, Oster, Dichio.

Having suffered the ignominy of being relegated to the bench in the previous seasons' Tyne-Wear derby defeat at St. James' Park, this was a game in which Alan Shearer was no doubt desperate for revenge, but the fixture would bring an even greater heartbreak that would haunt the United striker for years!

Unusually for the modern game, both captains were born locally; Alan Shearer in Gosforth and Micky Gray in Castletown on the outskirts of Sunderland. A packed St. James' Park was in full voice as United began the game attacking the Leazes End and within 18 seconds they should have been celebrating the opening goal when Speed was sent clear only to slice his shot wide from a great position. However, the Welsh captain soon made amends three minutes later when he opened the scoring. Solano created the goal with a terrific cross from the right and when Speed's header came back off the post, he swiveled to hook the rebound past Sorensen.

Sunderland were rocking at this stage and were fortunate not to fall further behind when a Speed header brought an excellent save from Sorensen. Then United won a free-kick out on the left which was curled to the far post where Acuna had taken up a great position, but the United midfielder could only succeed in sending his header into the side netting.

QUINN NETS THE WINNER

DON HUTCHISON CELEBRATES HIS EQUALISING GOAL

> "I KNOW IT'S JUST THREE POINTS, BUT IT'S A FANTASTIC RESULT FOR OUR FANS.
>
> My players showed tremendous character because we had to dig deep to get a foothold. Alan Shearer's normally deadly from the spot and I thought we were heading for an exciting last few minutes at 2-2, but Thomas pulled off a magnificent save. He showed he's a top-class 'keeper."
>
> PETER REID

> "ANT AND DEC, STING, ALAN SHEARER, SIR JOHN HALL, JIMMY NAIL, DONNA AIR, BOBBY ROBSON, ROBSON GREEN, TONY BLAIR. CAN YOU HEAR ME TONY BLAIR? YOUR BOYS TOOK ONE HELL OF A BEATING!"
>
> METRO RADIO'S SIMON CRABTREE AT THE FINAL WHISTLE

Soon afterwards, Sunderland were in with a chance when Thome's deep cross was headed down by Quinn and when Rae returned the ball, the big Irishman sent in a delicate chip from the edge of the box which brought a brilliant save from Given, the United 'keeper backpedaling to tip the ball over the bar. Then the visitors were desperately unlucky not to be awarded a penalty when Craddock looked a certain scorer from a left-wing free-kick only to be hauled to the ground by Shearer with referee Graham Poll waving away the desperate Sunderland appeals.

After a shaky start, Sunderland were very much back in the game in terms of possession, but were still trailing at the break with little evidence of the drama that was about to unfold in the second period. Just after the break, only a brilliant diving save by Given prevented Quinn's downward header giving Sunderland the lead, but the real turning point in the game came on 65 minutes when Peter Reid decided to sacrifice defender Chris Makin and bring on winger Julio Arca - the effect was immediate! Within two minutes Quinn took possession in the box and laid it wide to Phillips on the left who shrugged off the challenge of Hughes and crossed for Hutchison to volley home in some style at the far post.

With 16 minutes remaining, United came within a whisker of regaining the lead when a Solano free-kick came back into play off the woodwork with Sorensen nothing more than a spectator. The massed ranks of home supporters were still bemoaning their luck when Sunderland broke out of defence to score a goal of stunning quality. Rae began the move and when Arca dummied his pass, Gray raced down the left to send in a pin-point cross for Quinn to rise above the United defence and send a magnificent looping header into the net with Given beaten all ends up. It really was a superb finish by the Republic of Ireland international, described on 'Match of the Day' by Barry Davies that night as 'the most experienced head in the business'!

The 3,000 or so Sunderland fans high up in the stand behind the goal were celebrating wildly, but their joy turned to disbelief with eight minutes remaining when the home side appeared to have been given a reprieve after Quinn, back in his own penalty area, brought Lee crashing to ground with a clumsy challenge. Referee Graham Poll had no hesitation in awarding a spot-kick and the stadium held its breath as United's ace penalty-taker Alan Shearer stepped up to take the kick. The United skipper rarely missed from the spot, but this time his luck was out as Sorensen dived to his left to palm the ball away for a corner before being swamped by his delighted colleagues.

After that United were a spent force and at the final whistle there were wild celebrations among the Sunderland players with their ecstatic fans chanting 'We Always Win 2-1'.

THOMAS SORENSEN CELEBRATES VICTORY AT THE FINAL WHISTLE WITH EMERSON THOME

75

SUNDERLAND 2
CISSE (20) RICHARDSON (75)

NEWCASTLE UNITED 1
AMEOBI (30)

DATE: 25 October 2008
VENUE: The Stadium of Light
ATTENDANCE: 47,936
COMPETITION: Premier League
REFEREE: Mike Riley

SUNDERLAND: Fulop, Chimbonda, McCartney, Yorke, Ferdinand, Collins, Malbranque, Whitehead, Cisse, Diouf, Richardson.
SUBS: Colgan, Bardsley, Tainio, Leadbitter, Reid, Chopra, Jones.

NEWCASTLE UTD: Given, Beye, Bassong, Butt, Coloccini, Taylor, Geremi, Guthrie, Ameobi, Martins, Duff.
SUBS: Harper, Cacapa, Enrique, Barton, N'Zogbia, Gutierrez, Xisco.

It is doubtful whether Sunderland fans have ever enjoyed claiming the Tyne-Wear 'Bragging Rights' more than on this incredible afternoon of high drama at the Stadium of Light, that saw their team record a victory on home soil for the first time in 28 years! It was a game that had everything and some of it certainly wasn't pretty as tempers boiled over both on the pitch and on the terraces. On the day though, Sunderland were by far the better team and thoroughly deserved their victory over a disappointing Newcastle side.

Roy Keane's team quickly mastered the blustery conditions and deservedly took the lead on 20 minutes when Cisse thrust out a leg to divert Malbranque's driven cross-shot into the net, before racing away to celebrate in typical fashion with a double somersault!

Sunderland were very much in the driving seat at this stage, but ten minutes later United were level when Ameobi rose to head home Geremi's free-kick to stun the home crowd.

DJIBRIL CISSE CELEBRATES HIS OPENING GOAL

77

United could count themselves fortunate to be level at the interval and they appeared to be hanging on for a point until a moment of pure genius by Kieran Richardson won the points for Sunderland and almost lifted the roof off the Stadium of Light! The goal came from a free-kick just outside the box, hit with such power that the ball moved one way and then the other and was billowing in the back of the net before Given could move. It really was a stunning strike and it is doubtful whether the Stadium of Light has ever heard a louder roar than the one that exploded around the ground as the ball hit the net.

Sunderland could have added to their advantage soon afterwards when Cisse broke down the right to hit a terrific low drive that struck the far post before rebounding to safety. Then Jones, who had come off the bench to replace Yorke, missed a great chance when he headed over from close range with the goal at his mercy. With five minutes to go United brought on Joey Barton who had been on the receiving end of a fair amount of abuse from the home fans as he warmed up on the touchline. However, the former Manchester City man made little impact and soon afterwards, the final whistle signalled wild celebrations around the ground as well as some degree of disorder as the delirious Sunderland fans spilled onto the pitch.

> *"Football is an emotional game and it's been a while since our supporters had something to really celebrate. You've got to enjoy these things and I'm fully aware of the significance of overcoming our arch-rivals - I should be, I've been told about nine million times this week!"*
>
> ROY KEANE

KIERAN RICHARDSON'S THUNDERBOLT

NEWCASTLE UNITED 0
SUNDERLAND 3
SESSEGNON (27)   JOHNSON (74)   VAUGHAN (82)

DATE: 14 April 2013
VENUE: St. James' Park
ATTENDANCE: 52,355
COMPETITION: Premier League
REFEREE: Howard Webb

NEWCASTLE UTD: Krul, Debuchy, Gutierrez, Tiote, Taylor, Yanga-Mbiwa, Marveaux, Cabaye, Cisse, Sissoko, Gouffran.
SUBS: Elliot, Perch, Haidara, Anita, Ben Arfa, Campbell, Ameobi.

SUNDERLAND: Mignolet, Bardsley, Rose, N'Diaye, O'Shea, Cuellar, Johnson, Larsson, Graham, Sessegnon, McLean.
SUBS: Westwood, Kilgallon, Mangane, Colback, Vaughan, Laidler, Mandron.

If Paolo Di Canio is remembered for one thing during his relatively short stay in the Stadium of Light hot-seat, then it is almost certainly his ecstatic touchline celebrations as he punched the sky and slid along the muddy St. James' Park turf on his knees following his team's emphatic victory in this Tyne-Wear derby.

To mastermind such an important win in only his second game in charge was some achievement and it gave Sunderland's Premier League survival hopes a massive boost, while also dragging Newcastle into the relegation mire.

In typical derby fashion, it was the home side that made all the early running, but against the run of play, Sunderland had two penalty claims turned down by referee Howard Webb one of which looked clear-cut when Taylor pulled Danny Graham's shirt.

Then on 27 minutes, Di Canio's team grabbed the lead with a great goal from Stephane Sessegnon who received the ball 40 yards out and drove at the United defence before unleashing a terrific right-foot drive from the edge of the box that flew into the corner of the net!

SESSEGNON STARTS THE CELEBRATIONS

STEPHANE SESSEGNON

81

Newcastle responded immediately and Mignolet was soon called into action producing two excellent stops to deny Cisse. Then, just before the break Sunderland could have doubled their advantage when Cueller climbed highest to get in a powerful header from Larsson's corner, but Krul made an assured save. Soon afterwards however, the United 'keeper went down with a shoulder injury and was eventually replaced by Elliot.

Newcastle began the second half on the attack with Cisse proving to be a major threat to the Sunderland defence and just after the hour mark, he had the ball in the net only to see the effort wrongly ruled out for offside. It was a huge mistake by the linesman as replays later showed that Cuellar was clearly playing the United striker onside. It proved to be the turning point in the game.

Spurred on by their good fortune, Sunderland added a second with 15 minutes to go, this time a superb curling left-foot shot from the edge of the box from Adam Johnson. Then, with eight minutes remaining, David Vaughan made the game safe with another stunning strike. Receiving the ball on the left just outside the box, the Welsh midfielder unleashed a magnificent left-foot rising drive that flew into the far corner of the net with Elliot no more than a stunned spectator. The scenes that followed took some believing as Di Canio and his backroom staff joined in the ecstatic celebrations, while the disgruntled United fans streamed out of the ground. After the game there were angry exchanges outside St. James' Park with one United fan infamously attacking a police horse!

For Sunderland however, it had been a truly remarkable afternoon and the victory helped inspire a successful survival battle that saw the club preserve its Premier League status. For a while, the future prospects for the club looked encouraging under Di Canio, but after a poor start to the following campaign, the controversial Italian was shown the door. His spell as Sunderland boss was certainly brief, but also memorable for one very special afternoon on Tyneside!

> *"I wasn't nervous before the game because I believed in it, I believed we would win it. Let me reveal something to you that I normally wouldn't. On my way to the game, I saw the face of my Mama smiling at me - it's a year and a day since she passed way. I won a game at Swindon last year too, the day after she died, and I do not believe it was an accident that we won this game either. I believe in such things - I believe that things happen for a reason and I wanted to share my moment with the fans.*
>
> *"Mind you, these are the second pair of trousers I've ruined celebrating, but I would be happy to lose my trousers every week if we get a win."*
>
> **PAOLO DI CANIO**

82

PAOLO DI CANIO CELEBRATES AFTER DAVID VAUGHAN SCORES THE THIRD GOAL

SUNDERLAND 2
FLETCHER (5)   BORINI (84)

NEWCASTLE UNITED 1
DEBUCHY (57)

DATE: 27 October 2013
VENUE: The Stadium of Light
ATTENDANCE: 46,313
COMPETITION: Premier League
REFEREE: Lee Probert

SUNDERLAND: Westwood, Bardsley, Dossana, Cattermole, O'Shea, Cuellar, Larsson, Colback, Altidore, Fletcher, Johnson.
SUBS: Mannone, Celustka, Roberge, Gardner, Ki, Giaccherini, Borini.

NEWCASTLE UTD: Krul, Debuchy, Santon, Tiote, Williamson, Dummet, Sissoko, Cabaye, Remy, Ben Arfa, Gouffram.
SUBS: Elliot, Haidara, Anita, Obertan, Sammy Ameobi, Shoala Ameobi, Cisse.

Bottom of the table with only one point from their first eight games of the season, the odds were certainly stacked against Sunderland for this much-awaited encounter against their fiercest rivals. Yet on the day, new manager Gus Poyet's team produced an outstanding performance to secure an unlikely victory in front of a capacity crowd at the Stadium of Light.

Sunderland really couldn't have wished for a better start when Steven Fletcher opened the scoring with only five minutes on the clock. The goal came from a right-wing corner taken short by Johnson and when Larsson returned the ball, the England man whipped in a terrific cross for Fletcher to climb above Dummet at the far post and nod the ball home from a few yards out.

After that, the home side dominated proceedings with United's only worthwhile attempts coming from long-range and Westwood's only real first-half save coming from a Cabaye free-kick.

FLETCHER OPENS THE SCORING

The half-time break saw Newcastle boss Alan Pardew send on Cisse in place of Sissoko, no doubt in an attempt to improve his team's attacking threat, but they were unable to create anything during the opening exchanges of the second half despite enjoying the lion's share of possession. Then 12 minutes after the restart, they grabbed an unlikely equalizer when Ben Arfa drove the ball low across the goalmouth for Debuchy to convert at the far post.

The game was now on a knife edge and with 20 minutes remaining Poyet took the decision to bring on Fabio Borini in place of Adam Johnson. The impact was almost immediate as the Italian striker tested Krul with a fierce shot that the United 'keeper had to save at the second attempt.

Borini's attacking flare had certainly made a difference to the home side and with only six minutes remaining, he grabbed the winner with a stunning strike. Receiving the ball from Altidore 25 yards out he took a touch before unleashing a screaming right-foot shot high into the net that gave Krul no chance. It was a remarkable moment that had the Stadium of Light rocking as the celebrating Sunderland players became buried under a deluge of red and white supporters at the side of the pitch.

The noise in the stadium was unbelievable as the remaining few minutes were played out and was only silenced momentarily when a backward header from O'Shea almost gifted the Magpies an equaliser, but Westwood saved on the line under pressure from Cisse. Four minutes of time were added on, which Sunderland ran down by retaining possession and winning a succession of corners, before referee Lee Probert blew for time to bring the curtain down on a truly memorable victory.

> *"I remember everything about the goal, even the fans coming on and what they were wearing! It wasn't a great build-up, we were just trying to get the ball up the park because we were suffering, but I sniffed that I could get something. Obviously as a striker, when you're around the box you can sense things. It was a great lay-off by Jose and I just took a touch then hit it into the top corner.*
>
> *"When I saw their 'keeper wasn't going to reach it, I just went mad and raced to the corner flag. It was a great feeling and I got a few punches in the head, but that's OK!"*
>
> — FABIO BORINI

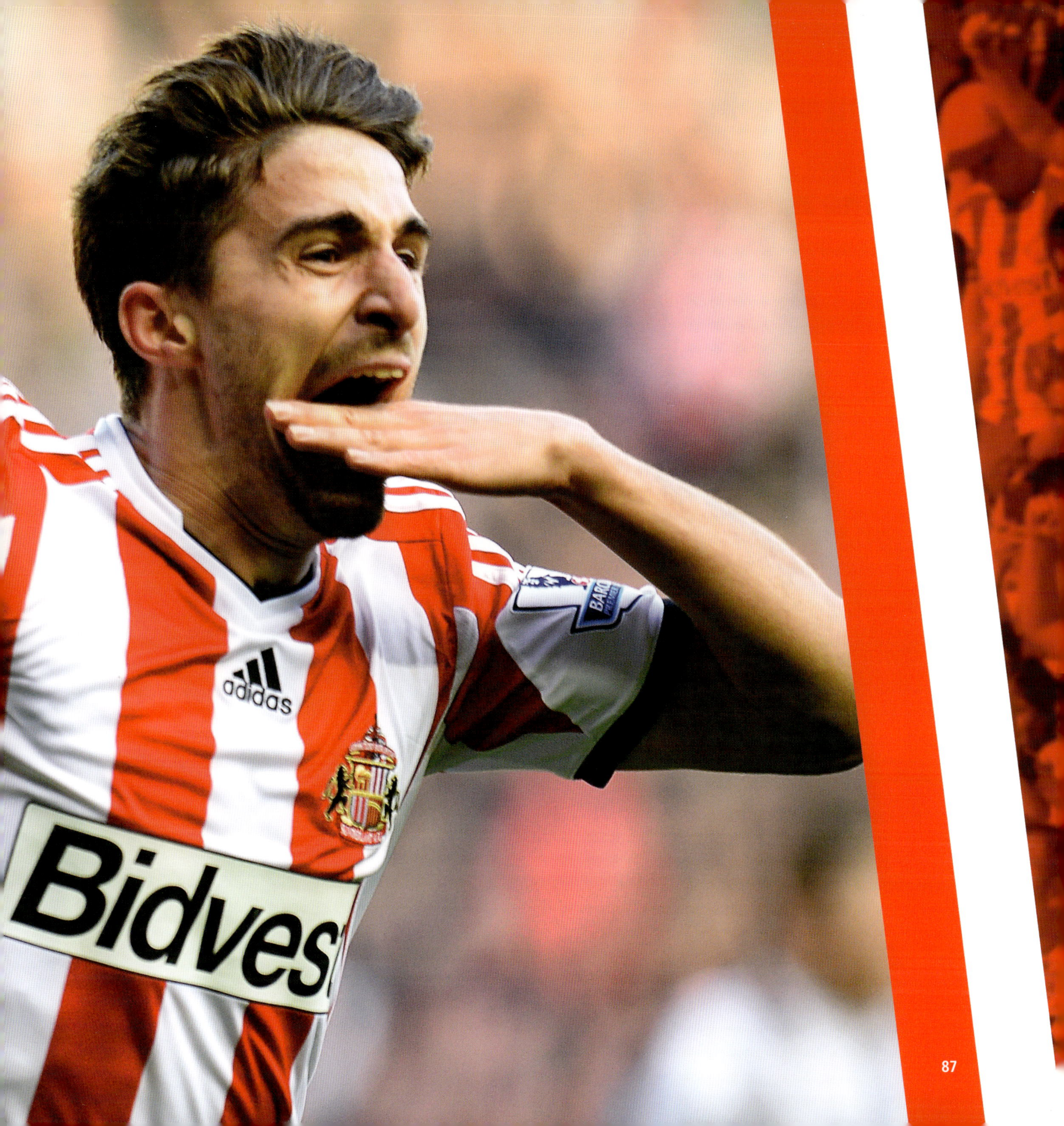
adidas

NEWCASTLE UNITED 0
SUNDERLAND 3
BORINI (19 PEN) JOHNSON (23) COLBACK (80)

DATE: 1 February 2014
VENUE: St. James' Park
ATTENDANCE: 52,280
COMPETITION: Premier League
REFEREE: Phil Dowd

NEWCASTLE UTD: Krul, Debuchy, Santon, Tiote, Williamson, Taylor, Sissoko, Anita, Shola Ameobi, Ben Arfa, Sammy Ameobi.
SUBS: Elliot, Haidara, Yanga-Mbiwa, Dummett, Marveaux, Armstrong, De Jong.

SUNDERLAND: Mannone, Bardsley, Alonso, Bridcutt, O'Shea, Brown, Johnson, Ki, Altidore, Colback, Borini.
SUBS: Ustari, Vergini, Gardner, Larsson, Giaccherini, Scocco, Wickham.

Sunderland were full value for this derby win in a game that saw Adam Johnson continue his recent fine form, prompting calls for his return to the England squad. United were never really in contention as Gus Poyet's team dominated the game from start to finish recording their third successive derby victory and equalling a record that had stood for 91 years!

After a slow start, the game burst into life when Sunderland were awarded a penalty after Anita fouled Bardsley in the box. Johnson had created the opening with a clever flick between two defenders to send Bardsley into the box only to be brought to the ground by Anita's clumsy challenge. It was a clear-cut decision for referee Phil Dowd who immediately pointed to the spot and Fabio Borini stepped up to drive the ball high into the net giving Krul no chance.

Soon afterwards the visitors doubled their advantage with a smart move down the left. Altidore's brilliant flick released Colback whose left-foot shot struck Taylor and ricocheted across the goal for Johnson to sweep the ball into an empty net at the far post. It was Johnson's sixth goal in four league games and he nearly added another early in the second half with a breathtaking piece of skill.

BORINI DELIGHTED AFTER HIS PENALTY

Receiving the ball out on the right just outside the penalty area, he brilliantly wriggled through a number of challenges before curling in a terrific left-foot shot that struck the post and rebounded to safety.

Sunderland were dominating proceedings now and Altidore should have netted a third when he was sent clear through the middle only to be denied by an excellent block by Krul. The United 'keeper had endured a busy afternoon, but he was powerless to prevent Sunderland's third goal, an assured finish by Jack Colback who won the ball on the half-way line and when he got it back on the left side of the penalty area, he drove a terrific shot high into the net.

The 3-0 scoreline certainly didn't flatter Sunderland who could easily have won the match by a greater margin. For their supporters, it was another fantastic afternoon on Tyneside and for the manager Gus Poyet, the satisfaction of becoming the first Sunderland manager to achieve a league double over Newcastle since Ian McColl achieved the feat back in 1967, ironically also with a 3-0 victory at St. James' Park!

GUS POYET

KI SUNG-YUENG

91

NEWCASTLE UNITED 0
SUNDERLAND 1
JOHNSON (90)

DATE: 21 December 2014
VENUE: St. James' Park
ATTENDANCE: 52,315
COMPETITION: Premier League
REFEREE: Anthony Taylor

NEWCASTLE UTD: Alnwick, Janmaat, Dummett, Tiote, Taylor, Coloccini, Gouffran, Colback, Perez, Sissoko, Sammy Ameobi.
SUBS: Woodman, Haidara, Williamson, Cabella, Riviere, Armstrong, Cisse.

SUNDERLAND: Pantilimon, Vergini, O'Shea, Cattermole, Coates, Brown, Johnson, Larsson, Fletcher, Gomez, Wickham.
SUBS: Mannone, Bridcutt, Rodwell, Buckley, Alvarez, Altidore.

Adam Johnson was once again the scourge of Tyneside as he netted a dramatic last-minute winner to extend Sunderland's run to four successive victories over the Magpies, an all-time record in Tyne-Wear derby matches.

Sunderland were forced to begin the game a substitute short after Reveillere was injured in the warm-up. The play was disappointing in the early exchanges with misplaced passes constantly hampering the progress of both teams, although Sunderland did improve as the first half progressed when they created three presentable chances. Fletcher was desperately unlucky when his volley struck the crossbar then Wickham wasted two excellent opportunities with his head.

There was a poignant moment on 17 minutes, both sets of supporters set aside their rivalries to pay tribute to Magpie fans Liam Sweeney and John Alder who had died on the Malaysia Airlines plane crash in July.

Apart from one strike from Sissoko, Newcastle had offered very little in the opening period, but they improved after the break and were near to breaking the deadlock when Perez forced a brilliant save from Pantilimon. Then, midway through the second-half, Taylor picked up a nasty facial injury after colliding with Fletcher and the post, although the United central defender was able to continue after treatment.

Throughout the game the home side had looked susceptible to the counter-attack and as the game entered the final minute they were caught out again, this time to devastating effect. With United piling men forward looking for the winner, Sunderland won possession allowing Johnson to set of on a great run from deep inside his own half and after shrugging off two challenges, he played the ball out to Fletcher on the left side of the United penalty area. The Sunderland centre-forward turned to pick out Buckley at the far post and when he laid the ball into Johnson's path, the winger took a touch before rifling the ball into the net. It was a goal of stunning quality created and finished by Johnson, a man very much on top of his game.

As the game moved into stoppage time, Larsson could have added a second when he broke through on the left, but from a difficult angle he only succeeded in firing his shot into the side netting. Moments later, the final whistle blew to bring down the curtain on another brilliant Sunderland derby victory on enemy soil.

STEVEN FLETCHER

94

"When he scored, I was just about to bring Adam Johnson off and put a defender on...

IT JUST SHOWS YOU HOW GOOD A COACH I AM!"

GUS POYET

SUNDERLAND 1
DEFOE (45)
NEWCASTLE UNITED 0

DATE: 5 April 2015
VENUE: The Stadium of Light
ATTENDANCE: 47,563
COMPETITION: League Division One
REFEREE: Mike Dean

SUNDERLAND: Pantilimon, Jones, Van Aanholt, Cattermole, Vergini, O'Shea, Defoe, Larsson, Fletcher, Gomez, Wickham.
SUBS: Mannone, Reveillere, Coates, Bridcutt, Buckley, Johnson, Graham.

NEWCASTLE UTD: Krul, Taylor, Colback, Gutierrez, Janmaat, Williamson, Cabella, Sissoko, Perez, Goufran, Sammy Ameobi.
SUBS: Elliot, Anita, Abeid, Kemen, Obertan, Armstrong, Riviere.

This Sunderland victory made it five Tyne-Wear derby wins in a row and also saw new manager Dick Advocaat repeat the feat of his predecessors, Gus Poyet and Paolo Di Canio, by celebrating a win over Newcastle in his second game in charge. However, on an otherwise disappointing afternoon, there was some good news for the Magpies as the game saw Jonas Gutierrez make his first appearance since August 2013 following his successful recovery from testicular cancer.

Played in an electric atmosphere throughout, this game was a stark contrast from Sunderland's previous home game when a 4-0 defeat by Aston Villa saw fans leave in their droves long before the end, a result that ultimately cost Gus Poyet his job. This time though, the fans stayed right to the end to cheer their team over the line following a nail-biting and hard-fought victory that saw no fewer than seven players receive yellow cards.

As Tyne-Wear derbies go, this was certainly no classic with few clear-cut chances being created by either side, but the goal that won it would stand comparison with any strike in the history of the fixture.

JERMAIN DEFOE

97

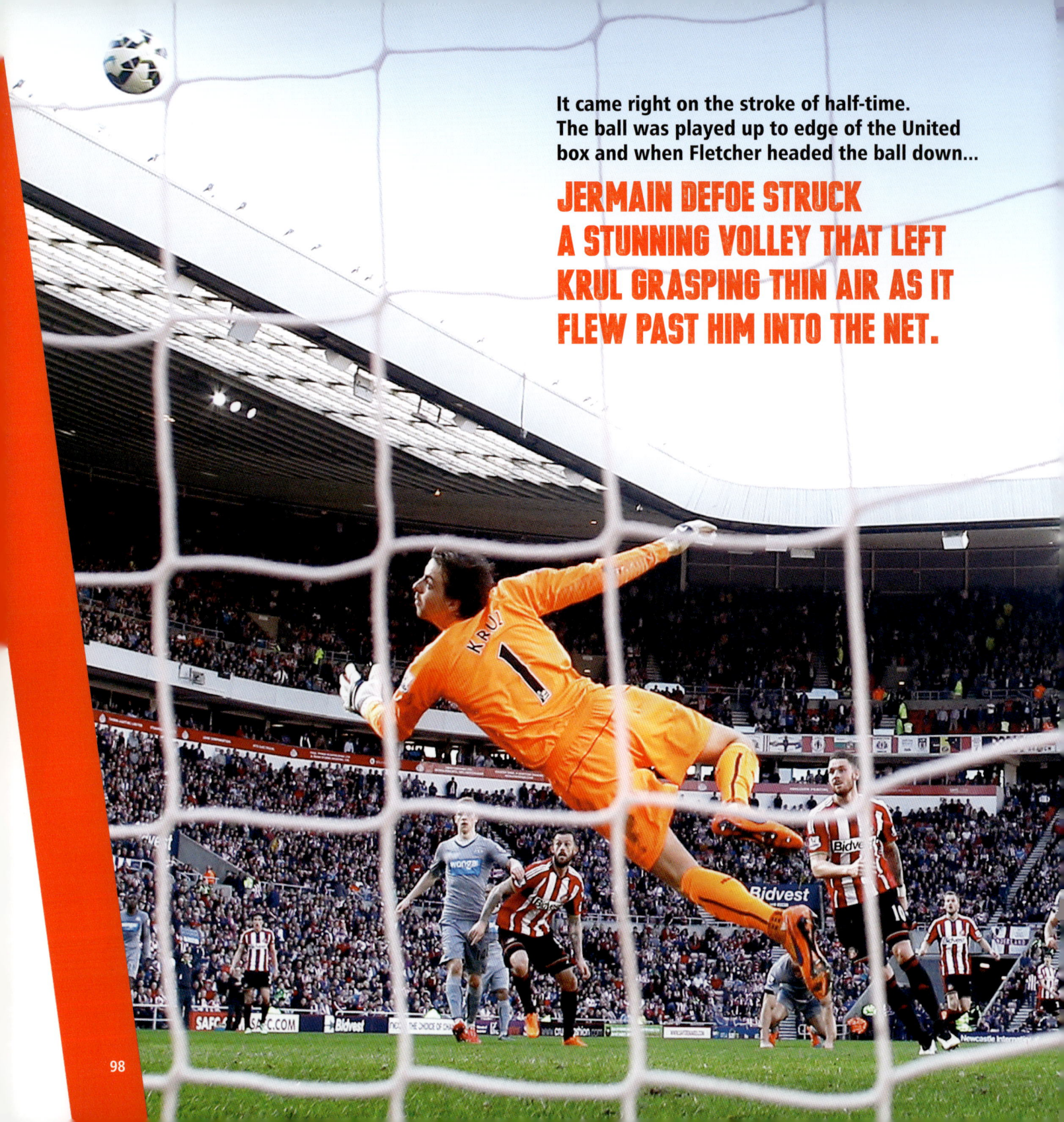

It came right on the stroke of half-time. The ball was played up to edge of the United box and when Fletcher headed the ball down...

JERMAIN DEFOE STRUCK A STUNNING VOLLEY THAT LEFT KRUL GRASPING THIN AIR AS IT FLEW PAST HIM INTO THE NET.

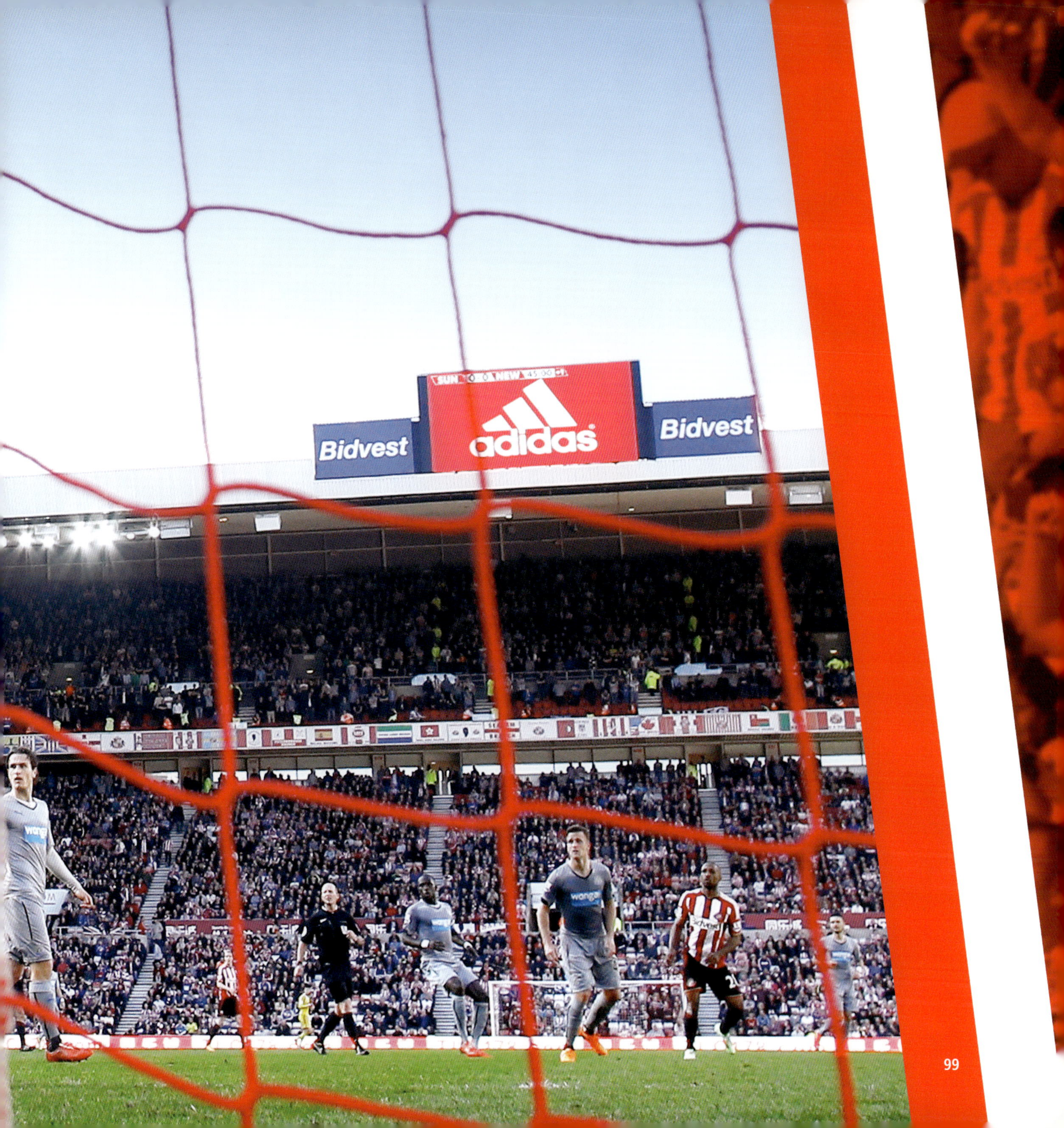
SUN 0 0 NEW 45:00
Bidvest
adidas
Bidvest

DICK ADVOCAAT

100

It was a moment of pure magic as Defoe raced away in celebration before finally coming to rest by sliding on his knees on the halfway line in front of the East Stand.

Almost immediately, the half-time whistle sounded with the Sunderland striker clearly in tears as he left the field. As he headed down the tunnel, the television cameras showed a smiling Tim Krul exchange a few words with Defoe, something that didn't go down too well with the United fans apparently!

The second half again saw Sunderland very much in control and Fletcher missed a great chance to double their advantage when he volleyed Gomez's cross over the bar. Then Van Aanholt shot wide from a decent position before Larsson curled a free-kick past the post.

United's late surge finally saw Pantilimon called into action with a smart save from Cabella, then three minutes from time Perez volleyed over from a corner. With that, the visitor's last chance of an equaliser had disappeared.

It had been a great team effort by Dick Advocaat's side who were made to fight every inch of the way for this victory, but for Sunderland fans, the game will always be remembered for Jermain Defoe's stunning winner, arguably the greatest goal ever scored in a Tyne-Wear derby!

"*Since I have been here, I have proven that I understand how big the club is and how much the people here love football. I also think I showed I am an emotional person after the goal went in. As the whistle went for half-time and as I was walking down the tunnel, I thought 'I'm crying and I'm on the telly' but I didn't care. For the fans and everyone it was just a special day. When you are a young kid playing football you want to play in massive games. The manager said to us beforehand, we were lucky to be playing in a game like this. There are so many young kids who wish they could play in a game like that. To be blessed enough and to score the winner is just amazing.*

"I have always been like this, but I think that's because I am old-school. Even when I have retired, I will probably still have a kick-about with my mates in the park. I love scoring goals and when I know it means so much to the fans, it just magnifies everything."

JERMAIN DEFOE

SUNDERLAND 3
JOHNSON (45 PEN) JONES (65) FLETCHER (86)
NEWCASTLE UNITED 0

DATE: 25 October 2015
VENUE: The Stadium of Light
ATTENDANCE: 47,653
COMPETITION: Premier League
REFEREE: Robert Madley

SUNDERLAND: Pantilimon, Yedlin, Jones, M'Vila, O'Shea, Kaboul, Johnson, Cattermole, Fletcher, Toivonen, Lens.
SUBS: Mannone, Van Aanholt, Coates, Larsson, Gomez, Watmore, Defoe.

NEWCASTLE UTD: Elliot, Janmaat, Dummett, Tiote, Coloccini, Mbemba, Sissoko, Colback, Mitrovic, Perez, Wijnaldum.
SUBS: Woodman, Haidara, Lascelles, Anita, Thauvin, De Jong, Cisse.

Sunderland made it 'Six in a Row' with this victory and just as his predecessors had done in the three previous derby matches, it was a win for new manager Sam Allardyce in only his second game in charge.

While the scoreline suggests a comfortable victory for Sunderland, it was anything but that, until a controversial incident right on the stroke of half-time changed the game completely. Up until then, the visitors had enjoyed the lion's share of possession and could count themselves unfortunate not to have grabbed the lead with a number of half-decent chances being missed.

Then, as the first-half drew to a close, Defoe sent Fletcher through on the left side of the box. Elliot might well have reached the ball first, but before he could, Coloccini inexplicably barged the Sunderland striker off the ball and referee Robert Madley immediately pointed to the spot before showing the United central-defender a red card. Initially it looked a very soft penalty, but replays suggested that the referee may well have called it correctly. Then up stepped Adam Johnson, so often a thorn in United's side in the past, to despatch the kick low into the corner of the net before racing the length of the pitch to celebrate in front of the black and white hordes in the North Stand.

...AND JOHNSON SCORES

FLETCHER IS FOULED FOR THE PENALTY...

103

M'VILA CELEBRATES GETTING THE SECOND GOAL

104

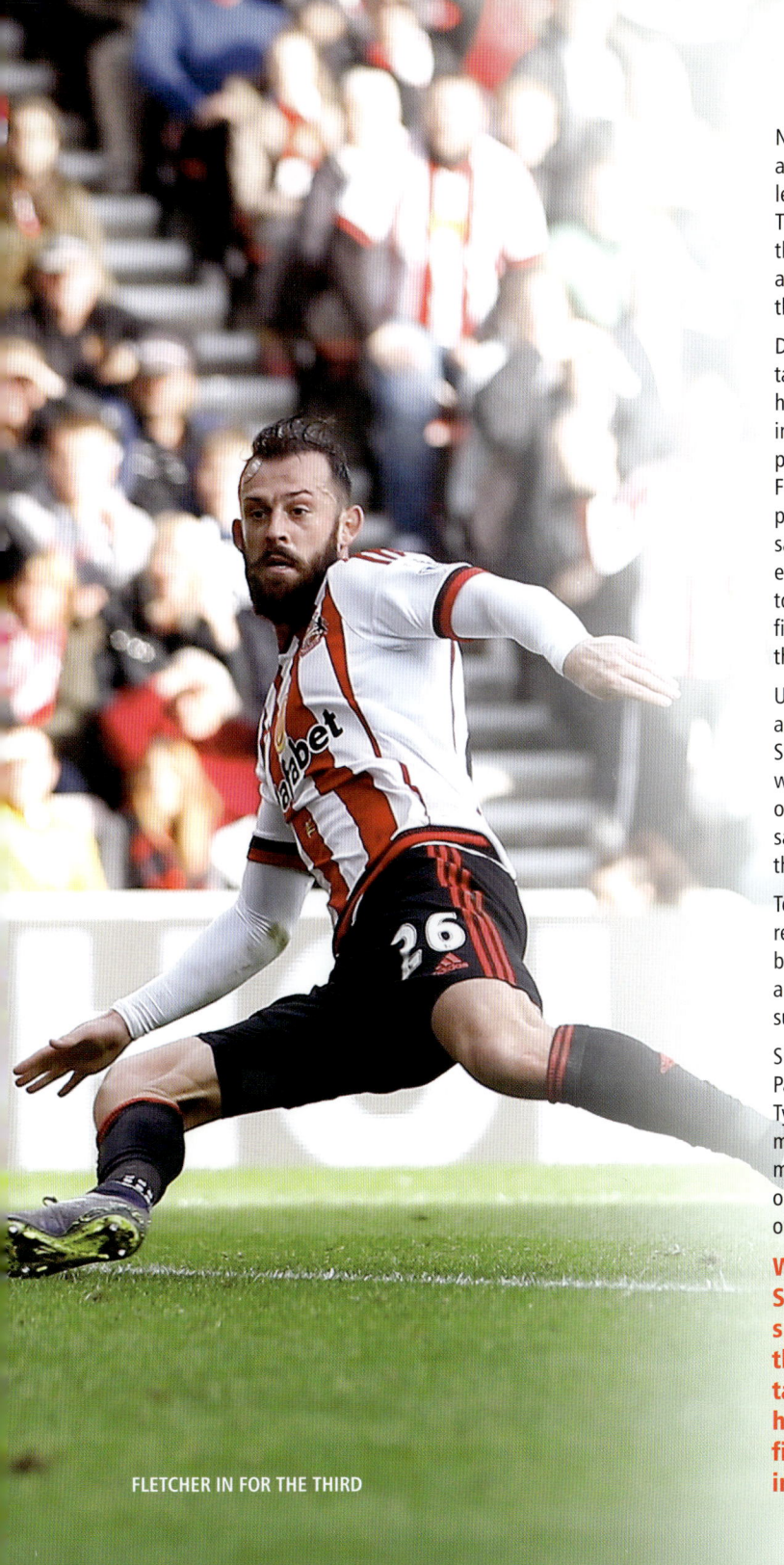

Newcastle's hopes of getting back into the game suffered a blow early in the second half when Colback was forced to leave the field following a strong challenge by Cattermole. The former Sunderland man received a torrent of abuse from the home fans as he walked around the perimeter of the pitch, although hardly attempting to diffuse the situation by kissing the badge on his shirt!

Despite their man advantage, Sunderland were still struggling to take control of the game and ten minutes into the half Mitrovic had a great chance to level the scores. Controlling the ball brilliantly in the box, he turned to beat his man, but failed to get any real power in his shot allowing Pantilimon to make a comfortable save. Fortune had certainly favoured Sunderland and they finally began to push forward looking for a goal that would probably make the game safe. Then on 64 minutes, Fletcher sent in a terrific effort from the edge of the box that was heading for the top corner until a deflection took it over the bar. From the resulting corner however, Sunderland finally doubled their advantage when M'Vila sent in a terrific volley that was turned into the net by Billy Jones from close range.

Undeterred, the visitors still pressed forward and came close when an excellent shot by Perez was turned behind by Pantilimon. The Sunderland 'keeper then flapped at the corner kick before the ball was finally scrambled clear. Then the play switched quickly to the other end where Johnson came within a whisker of making the game safe when he cut in from the right to unleash a beautifully struck shot that Elliot just managed to fingertip onto the bar.

To their credit, the visitors were still battling, but with four minutes remaining, Sunderland killed the game following some excellent play by Kaboul. The central defender picked the ball up inside his own half and advanced towards United's depleted defence before producing a sublime cross for Fletcher to volley home with some style at the far post.

Sunderland's run of derby victories finally came to an end at St. James' Park a few months later when they were held to a 1-1 draw, but the Tyne-Wear rivalry certainly wasn't over for another season by any means. Both clubs were deep in relegation trouble as the season moved into its final week with Sunderland, incredibly, having a great opportunity to dump their rivals into the Championship with a victory over Everton in their final home game.

With the Stadium of Light packed to the rafters, Sam Allardyce's team romped home with a 3-0 victory sparking huge celebrations at the final whistle with the manager and his players returning to the pitch to take the plaudits of the fans with a memorable lap of honour. If ever the Tyne-Wear bragging rights lay firmly in Sunderland hands, then it was on that truly incredible night of high drama at the Stadium of Light!

FLETCHER IN FOR THE THIRD

SAM ALLARDYCE CELEBRATES WITH THE FANS

THE ROKER END, 5 APRIL 1980